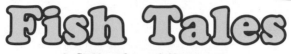

Fish Tales

**A Collection of Humorous
Fishing Stories**

Fish Tales

A Collection of Humorous Fishing Stories

Alan Liere

Northwest Fly Fishing, LLC
Seattle, Washington

NORTHWEST
Fly Fishing

SOUTHWEST
Fly Fishing

EASTERN
Fly Fishing

www.matchthehatch.com

Published by
NORTHWEST FLY FISHING, LLC
600 1st. Ave., Ste. 512
Seattle, WA 98104
www.matchthehatch.com

Distributed by
STACKPOLE BOOKS
5067 Ritter Road
Mechanicsburg, PA 17055
www.stackpolebooks.com

Printed in China

First edition

10 9 8 7 6 5 4 3 2 1

ISBN-10: 0-9779454-1-3
ISBN-13: 978-0-9779454-1-2

Library of Congress Control Number: 2008934116

"My experience has taught me that a man who has no vices has damned few virtues."

Abraham Lincoln

The Permission-Seeker

Contents

Foreword

If Alan Liere isn't the funniest writer in the world today, he's a contender for the position. I personally know of no writer who can surpass him. The fact that he aims his humor mostly at an outdoor audience restricts him considerably, but there can be no better audience, no more appreciative audience, than those of us who hunt and fish. Al knows us like his favorite trout stream, every ripple and boulder.

In the mid-1970s, Al walked into my writing workshop and announced to me and the assembled graduate students that he had written a humor piece. There is no announcement from a student that a writing professor dreads more. Normally, this audience will greet the reading of the announced "humor" piece with stony silence. By the time the critiques begin, the hopeful "humorist" will have shriveled up into a pale little creature who will never again attempt to write humor or, quite possibly, anything else. When Al read his piece aloud, however, the students exploded into uncontrolled, gut-busting laughter. That story, about a classic date from hell, was one of the funniest I have ever heard or read.

It is very difficult to break into the magazine market with a humor story because editors are afraid of humor. They may laugh themselves prostrate over a piece and then stuff it into an envelope to the writer, along with a rejection slip. Editors fear they may be the only ones who think the piece is funny, and there is no bit of prose more terrible than a humor piece that isn't funny. They are reluctant to take the chance, worried about what the reader will think of them if the piece really isn't all that good. The fact that Al has somehow overcome this editorial prejudice and has managed to sell thousands of humor pieces to magazines and newspapers attests to the high quality of his work.

A strange kind of comic wisdom runs through much of Alan Liere's writing. Al's humor is, from time to time, very serious. Mostly, though, and fortunately for those of us who love comedy, Al is most often hilariously funny. It is a rare talent, and I hope this book sells 10 million copies, not for Al's sake but for the sake of all the readers out there who need a laugh to help get them through the day.

Patrick F. McManus

Author's Note

As the author of a fly-fishing book, I have a terrible confession to make: I am neither a fly-fishing nor a trout-fishing purist. The truth is, I like to catch fish—not just cast for them—and I will chase anything that will put a bend in my rod. If dunking a nightcrawler will bring me more walleye action than drifting a size-14 Adams, that's what I will do. I would cast fermented chicken lips on a size-2 hook if that were the difference between catfish fillets and fried Spam for breakfast; for you see, I take immense pleasure in preparing and eating some of what I catch, and I find members of the spiny-rayed species oh so delectable, and oh so vulnerable to bait.

Let's face it—while every species of fish will at some point take a fly, for some it's too darn much work just to prove a point. Yes, it would be nice to tell my friends I hooked an 80-pound halibut on a fly, but I'd much rather land that fish and then serve them halibut steaks while recalling my fly-fishing experience with huge rainbow on Alaska's Kenai River.

There! It is done. Now, if there are members of an exclusive fly-fishing fraternity who wish to hang me by my unmentionables, so be it. I will not, however, go gently. I am, above all, a fisherman, and while fly-fishing is my favored method of pursuit, I am not so silly as to believe anglers who don't know a White-Butted Skunk from a stinky brown ferret are going to hell.

Many fly fishermen view their sport as a philosophical confrontation between a man and a fish—something that occurs in cosmic isolation. As you may have guessed, I also view this idea, like the conclusions of so many other philosophical inquiries, as hogwash. Fishing brings people into contact with other people—partners, guides, wives, and offspring—even the unknown and unwanted stranger on the far bank who is intent on fishing the best pool.

Nevertheless, in the solitude of a lake or stream, when the crowds have all gone home and quiet settles on the water like a spinner fall, the fisherman often strikes up a conversation with himself. For me, this has been both frightening and enlightening. I have come to know myself while fishing, and perhaps even better by recalling and then writing these stories. If, in the process, I have brought amusement or introspection or happy reminiscing.or laughter to others, my purpose is complete. I think my publisher would like to sell a whole bunch of these books, though. You can make us all happy if you buy a couple dozen.

Alan Liere
July, 2008

The Permission-Seeker

◆

D uring my years as a permission-seeker, I've been refused, humiliated, horrified, and hurt. This year, however, my endeavors reached a new, painful low.

While scouting fishing water along the Colville River, I chanced upon a farm home where a clear feeder creek ran practically through the front yard. Even from my car, I could see finning brown trout. Keenly aware that this was a very good sign, I went to the door.

"Ma'am," I said, when a short, white-haired lady came to the door, "I was just driving by and I noticed…"

"Seldon!" she called over her shoulder, "We got us some company!"

Seldon came up slowly to grin at me over his wife's shoulder. He looked very much like his wife but he wasn't wearing lipstick. "Howdy-do," he said pleasantly. "You come to look at pigs?"

"Well, actually," I said, "I was hoping to get permission to fish."

Seldon's face dropped. This was not good. As a veteran permission-seeker, I knew I had muddied the waters too quickly.

". . . but I'm also very interested in pigs," I lied. "Perhaps after I look at your pigs we can talk about fly fishing." With that, Seldon and his wife carried me in their wake from the back porch to a fenced pasture where no fewer than 60 pigs lined up to greet us.

"That's Bitsy," Seldon said, pointing out a bristly-haired male that looked like a mutated wiener dog. "He's quite the cutup."

"Yes," said his wife. "And that's Dwayne, his first son. Dwayne is quite the card himself. He can really get the bunch stirred up."

"Oh, I'll bet he can," I said, staring longingly across the pasture where the stream cut through a patch of willows.

"We like Dwayne's haunches," said Seldon. "He's thick, but he's long, too. Here," he said, extending his hand to bring the animal nearer, "just feel the thickness."

"Mmmmm," I said. "Thick."

"Dwayne wants to kiss you," the lady said. "See how he's cocking his head. Just stick your face over the fence, mister, and I'll bet you can kiss him."

"Couldn't we just shake hands?" I mumbled. Nevertheless, I knew the rules of permission-seeking, so I closed my eyes and stuck my face over the fence. Dwayne snorted, lassoing my eyebrows and nose with a great gob of hog slobber.

"Oh my," Seldon said. "Dwayne must still have a cold."

In the next hour, I learned the names of and a fair amount of genealogy about every animal in the herd. I also learned more about the intimate habits and personal hygiene of pigs than I ever wanted to know.

"Uh—Seldon," I finally ventured when it appeared the "tour" was winding down, "about those trout. You think maybe I could come out next weekend and fish that little creek in your front yard?"

"Fish?" Seldon asked. "My creek?" He glared at me suspiciously. Then, he grinned real big. "Say," he said, "You haven't seen our banty chickens! You just got to come over to the hen house and look at our banties."

CHADWELL '08

Fishin' Hats

When I was a kid, every adult male in my father's generation wore a fedora. I saw an old photo once, circa 1940, taken during a company picnic at a local amusement park, and there wasn't an uncovered male head in the bunch. When my father and relatives gathered, it always reminded me of pictures I had seen of Eliot Ness and Chicago mobsters. The only thing missing were the machine guns.

Thankfully for me, my father wore two kinds of hats—a fedora, when he wasn't fishing, and a porkpie when he was. The porkpie, of course, was my favorite, as it was decorated with all sorts of feathery and bug-eyed creations, and when Dad put it on, I knew good times were a-comin'.

Sometime in the late '50s, Dad quit wearing fedoras. Neighbors began sporting baseball caps for just about any event, but my father thought baseball caps looked silly on anyone other than baseball players, and he started wearing the old porkpie fly-fishing hat for every outdoor occasion except church picnics.

Then, as now, there did not seem to be any rules involved in wearing baseball caps. You were just as likely to see them in the audience at a formal wedding, on the beach, or at any dinner table but ours. My father never wore his porkpie in the house, and did not allow baseball caps at our dinner table, no matter who was wearing them. He'd have loved to have invited Mickey Mantle to take supper with us, but even Mickey would have first been required to remove his cap.

Today, I wear a baseball cap on occasion, but never to play baseball.

Mostly, I wear a replica of Dad's old porkpie hat when I am fly fishing to prevent my balding knob from getting burned. I tried sticking a few flies in it to emulate my father, but somehow my efforts seemed contrived, an attempt to be a codger, and I am not yet ready for the codgerdom my father embraced. Other than that, I wear caps or stocking hats only when I haven't had time to comb my hair (such as it is), though I find this problem can be more permanently resolved with an electric dog clipper set on low.

Unlike my father, I have tried to be more forgiving of those who still wear their baseball caps inside, but just when I thought I had perhaps gained a modicum of tolerance, they started wearing them backwards! Then, they started wearing them sideways! Sideways, a baseball cap screams DOOFUS!

For Father's Day six years back, my son gave me a felt, fedora-type hat. I was planning a fly-fishing trip to Chile at the time, and he thought I should make an attempt to be stylish. It was a very nice hat, really, and I did wear it in Chile. It shielded me from the rain and sun and made me feel ever so competent. I missed my porkpie, though, and my guide wore a baseball cap—sideways!

Last week, for the first time ever, I saw a baseball cap I actually liked. It is a plain dark blue, and stapled to the back just inside the adjustment band is a long, gray ponytail that matches my own hair perfectly. I think my father, who had a great sense of humor, would have worn that one fishing just for the hell of it. I think I will, too. There's a little stretch of creek only 20 minutes from here owned by an old hippie who won't let anyone on his property. I think he might appreciate my new look.

Fishin' Hats • 11

Sn-n-a-a-a-kes

❧

When I was a youngster, nothing could hold a candle to the lingering horror generated by settling deep into a musty sleeping bag on my grandmother's screened back porch and letting that white-haired lady scare me with stories about snakes. Long after she had put me to bed, I would lie there alone, listening for dry, slithery sounds on the linoleum, thinking about all sorts of terrible, death-dealing serpents.

Oddly enough, while Grandma's snake stories scared me, snakes themselves did not, and, as I was growing up, I not only accepted their presence, I was fascinated by it. Still, it was not until a few years ago that I realized how useful snakes could be.

It was August and I had been camping for a week just outside of Navajo Dam in New Mexico. Most of the days had been spent casting size-6 grasshoppers to rainbows on the San Juan River, but this morning, just for a change, I'd been throwing homemade spongebugs to big bluegills on a hidden three-acre pond I'd discovered south of Route 550. When it got too hot for comfort, I kept a couple of fish for lunch, threading them on a willow stringer. Then I climbed up to the road, practically into the arms of a sweating, heavy-set man who had been watching my progress from his car.

"So that's where that sunfish hole's at!" he exclaimed. "Woulda never thought to look so close to home." Already, he was pulling a spinning rod and a can of night crawlers from the backseat. "Heck, I didn't even know there was water back there," he added, getting out of the car.

"Ahhh, mister," I began, "it's a real small pond. If you keep too many there won't be any..."

"Ya woulda done a lot better with worms," the man said. "Them foo-foo artificials might be OK fer trout, but fer sunfishes ya need worms."

I was about to make my plea from a different angle when he gushed, "Can't wait to bring Cleon and Rufus. We'll have us a real fish fry!" Grinning, he hiked up his trousers and disappeared over the bank. "Got just the thing," he mumbled. "Gonna catch every damn..."

"Watch out for snakes," I said quietly.

There was a silence of perhaps 10 seconds, and I knew the man had stopped walking. Then, rocks began to clatter and his head reappeared, the eyes rather pleasantly fearful, the mouth pursed tightly but twitching just a little. "Sn-n-a-a-a-a-kes?" he said, the word rising in tone as he forced it from his chest.

"Western diamondbacks and sidewinders," I offered. "The usual. There's lots of em." I leaned back against his car and chewed nonchalantly at a thumbnail, feeling very fine. It really didn't matter if venomous pit vipers or harmless bull snakes or nothing at all guarded my pond. And it didn't matter, either, how many there were or weren't. Obviously, the mere thought of one snake, any variety, was too many.

His face frozen in bug-eyed terror, the man sort of tiptoed back toward me. "That was a mean thing to tell me, mister," he said angrily. He made one final, rather graceless leap, grabbing for the car door in midair and flinging himself inside, huffing. "You probably ain't never seen a single snake the whole time."

"So why aren't you fishing, then?" I asked smugly.

"Cause you mighta," he whined. He threw his rod into the backseat and slid over behind the wheel. With an offended glare, he drove off.

Grandma would have been delighted, but I almost felt sorry for him.

The Dual

❖

It should have been another pleasant afternoon of winter steelheading. A bright sun warmed my back, and though I was enjoying my own company, I didn't begrudge the stranger who walked down the bank to stand beside me.

Tying on a weighted Skykomish Sunrise, he cast it upstream, expertly bouncing it from rock to rock. Almost immediately, he was tied to a flashy male, and I watched the battle with more interest than envy. I had learned years ago that I was destined to catch fewer fish than others, and while I had accepted this malediction gracefully, I did need to be the best at something. I compensated, therefore, by building prodigious, quality lunches, taking enormous pride in eating all I wanted and still being the last on the river with some gourmet tidbit or another.

I pulled a salami and rye from my coat pocket and took a bite. Seeing this, the stranger quickly landed and released his fish. Then he produced a smoked cheese ball, which he carefully sliced atop his tackle box. Next, he set up a one-burner stove and began to boil water. "Mocha," he said. "Nothing like hot mocha when it's cold on the river."

"You said it," I said, reaching for the apple in my cooler. Before it was in my mouth, he was deftly dissecting a kiwi fruit.

"Hard to get good kiwi these days," he said.

"Right," I replied, digging for my Double-Stuff Oreos.

Immediately, the stranger countered with a huge slice of pecan pie. Somehow, it was still steaming.

"You fish here often?" I asked a few minutes later. His pie was gone and he was fishing again.

"Some," he huffed, setting the hook with one hand and reaching for a box of Dutch sesame crackers with the other.

"You're good, mister," I said. Hoping to surprise him, I whipped out a turkey drumstick, and then a box of powdered donuts. He countered immediately with ham croquettes and a mammoth hunk of burnt-chiffon cake. The fish stayed on.

An hour went by during which I ate only pepperoni sticks while he wolfed down raspberry bombe and marinated artichokes.

"You're not done are you?" he called gleefully. I shrugged. "I knew it," he whooped. "Haven't seen the man yet who could out-lunch me." He threw open his cooler. "Guess I might as well clean up the smoked almonds."

He dove in, smacking and grunting like a hog under an apple tree, but just as he finished, he caught the glint of metal. Towering above him pointing a stainless steel Thermos at his bloated belly, I did my best John Wayne. "Yer outta business, pilgrim," I drawled, cocking my thumb above the container of hot French vichyssoise. Then, I flung open my second cooler—the full one I had been sitting on. I extracted a ginger-sauced beef tongue. "You'd best show yer heels."

Just before the sun dipped behind Mt. Quincy, the stranger did just that. Sundown, I thought. Out of town by sundown. I could never catch a steelhead after dark, but I knew it didn't matter. A man doesn't have to be the best at everything.

Tuff Enuff

From the very beginning, I have been an easy mark for fly shop owners who exalt a product's toughness. I think this conundrum began when, at 10 years of age, I bought my first rod from Bobby Sherman across the alley. There was nothing particularly wonderful about Bobby's old glass Eagle Claw, except that Bobby's father had run over it with his tow truck, and that, in my eyes, made it the best fly rod ever.

In like manner, my first reel, a scarred single-action, was used mainly as a projectile by a neighborhood widow who would heave it at the sparrows that sat on her clothesline, plotting their assault on her cherry tree. Despite the abuse, it still maintained some fly-reel-like characteristics, and I bought it for a buck. I figured anything with that kind of stamina had to be worth at least a buck.

This toughness criterion wasn't a mere childhood disorder, either. Long past puberty, I purchased a float tube because the salesman convinced me it was so rugged it would bounce back even if a piano were dropped on it from 40 feet up. Why would I care if my float tube could withstand that kind of abuse? I can hardly remember the last time I had to dodge a piano while fishing. A neighbor, Burton Ells, had his canoe sink on Eloika Lake back in '59, but he was pretty sure it was a beaver-felled cottonwood that did the damage. Burton had been sucking on a bottle of Old Factory Whistle (one blast and you're through for the day), and he wasn't too clear about the details.

Fly boxes are also a problem. When I was 15, I bought my first from a company that promised it would never crack or warp. It didn't, either. What I needed, though, was one that wouldn't float off or sink, even when I was upside down in the Green River.

I once purchased a pair of hip waders because the advertisement suggested they were impervious to tears. For the most part, they were. Primarily this was because they were composed of a space-age road-surfacing material and weighed approximately 23 pounds each. Fall out of a boat with those babies on, and you didn't have to worry about swimming because you could walk to shore on the bottom of the lake.

But it all comes back to fly rods; that's where most of my money is. I'm a sucker for those that can be bent tip to butt; I have owned several. As claimed, they have survived electric car windows, airport baggage handlers, and even my sister-in-law's children, but I don't think a rod exists that can withstand the persistence of a teething Lab pup. Certainly none of mine.

Nine years ago, the finest fishing opportunity I almost ever had was ruined when I eagerly sprang from a chartered helicopter onto a gravel bar on a trout river in the mountains of southern Utah. Just as my feet hit the ground, the rotating blades lopped off the first 30 inches of my new Loomis and flung it into oblivion. The pilot said I was lucky it wasn't my head, but that didn't ease the pain of spending a once-in-a-lifetime afternoon with a 5-foot rod casting to 3-foot rainbow cruising the surface just out of my diminished casting range.

This last fiasco depressed me so badly that when I got home, I scheduled a one-hour session with Dr. Scrueluse, a behavioral therapist. He told me the seed for my depression stemmed from a chromosomatic enervation rather than an acquired neurosis exacerbated by immoderation. Then he presented me with a bill for $150. I suggested the doctor take a flying leap off something really, really high. I figured if he survived the fall, he had to be worth the money.

A Paid Vacation

❖

Aweek after I completed my sophomore year in high school, my father crept down the basement stairs to where I was happily tying my summer's supply of Carey Specials. "Guess what, Alan," he said, blocking the only exit, "Lester is here."

My head jerked up from my fly vise. Slow to mature, I had already decided Fords and females were unimportant enough to support by working. The Little Spokane River was within biking distance of my home, and I had purposely kept my life uncomplicated so that I could spend nonschool hours fishing. My father had mentioned he knew a man, Lester Simms, who would give me a summer job, but I didn't want a job and had not considered Dad's revelation threatening.

For a big man, my father was quick. He grabbed me by one heel as I attempted to propel myself through a basement window. Then, he hauled me outside in a headlock to where a man I had never before seen was holding a packed blue duffel I recognized as mine. "Son," my father said, loosening his hold just enough for me to look up, "this is Lester Simms. Lester has a spread north of here. You'll be spending the summer with him—$250 a month and your room and board."

"Pleased to meet ya," Lester smiled, bending down to look into my reddening face. "You goin' peaceful, or you gonna ride in back with Satan?" He jerked his thumb toward the bed of a 1 1/2-ton truck where a very large, very untidy Hereford bull was in the process of adding to his unsanitary confinement. "You might be more comfortable up front with me."

When Dad released his grip and tried to talk to me, I shrugged him off and climbed into the truck cab where I glared down, resigned to hating him for three months. Finally, Lester got in, too, but he just sat there quietly.

"You ever change a line of sprinklers or buck bales?" he said at last. "No," I said snottily, as if the question offended me.

Lester slapped me enthusiastically on the knee. "That's good! I sure don't need somebody who knows more'n me." Then, he became more subdued. "Tell me, boy, what do you like?"

For the first time since we'd met, I looked at Lester Simms. Did I dare tell him about freedom—about morning smells on the Little Spokane River, the way it talked to me as it raced under the golf course bridge? "Just fishin'," I said simply.

Lester brightened. "Fishin'!" he boomed. "That's just what yer old man told me. Didja bring yer rod?"

I studied him curiously. "What for?"

"Boy," Lester laughed, "you ain't gonna spend every minute of every day workin'. Why, I got a quarter mile on the Colville River. We got rainbow and brown trout both." He whistled. "Whoo-ee do we got brown trout. Now you run in the house and get your rod."

Like a shot, I was out of the cab, racing up the front walk. My father was sitting on the porch smiling, and I stopped awkwardly before him.

"Funny, isn't it," he said, "how things have a way of getting better?" He put his hand on my shoulder and squeezed. "Now, go find us some monster browns. I'll be out weekends."

The Things My Father Told Me

❖❖❖

Friends of mine who did not know my father are puzzled that his memory is still so much a part of my life. Dad died almost 10 years ago, at 83 years of age, you see, and, at 60, I'm not exactly a dependent son. I guess my friends figure that instead of forever relating Walter Liere lore, I should be out there creating some lore of my own. "Do you just want to be remembered as the son of Walt Liere?" they ask me.

"That wouldn't be so bad," I tell them.

When I was a kid, I never doubted my father was the tallest and smartest man in the world. By the time I became an adult, I knew he was also the kindest, most forgiving, most generous, and most wise.

That my trust in this man was complete is illustrated by an incident that occurred when I was 7. We were camping and fishing, as we often did, and Mom had barbecued pork chops for dinner. I asked my father to identify the gelatin-like substance found in the little indentation at the back of my pork chop bone. Without pause, Dad told me it was the pig's brains. Thirty years later, married and with children of my own, I was again sitting at a campground picnic table sucking happily on a pork chop bone. Suddenly, I was struck with a revelation. "Brains?" I exclaimed. "How can this be brains?"

Dad told me other things too, fun, harmless tidbits that I eventually discovered weren't exactly accurate—like what you call the brown substance secreted by a grasshopper, how peacock herl originated, and where tadpoles, spittle bugs, and dragonflies come from. I was probably the only kid in the whole world who spent an afternoon fishing through the grate of a city sewer because my dad told me there were fish down there. He didn't do it to be mean, though—he did it because I desperately wanted to go fishing and he couldn't get time off from work to take me. He suspected that as long as I had a fishing rod in my hand I would be happy, and he was right. It wasn't as euphoric as casting dry flies to 18-inch cutthroat, mind you, but it beat playing house with my sister.

Once in a while, as I tumbled through my teens, I ignored my father's advice. Ignoring fatherly advice is almost an obligation for a son whose voice is still changing. It always cost me, though.

"Never loan your fly rod to a friend," he told me, so I loaned my fly rod to a friend and ended up with an ex-friend and a broken fly rod. "Take the time to do it right," he said, so I hurried through and had to do it twice. "Admit your deficiencies and call an expert," he told me. So I tried to do it myself, and the reel fell apart with a 10-pound brown on the line. Then the tip broke. So did my heart. It was my first cane rod.

As an adult, I still need my father to remind me about stitches in time and counting chickens before they're hatched and birds in the hand being better than birds in the bush. This world is changing rapidly, but I wouldn't mind having him around to point the way. Dad didn't know a modem from a gigabyte, but he possessed common sense, he knew and practiced the basics of decency, and he could read the water like nobody's business. In questions of love, manners, morals, finance, friendship, and fishing, Dad always had the right answers.

The Way to Go Home

Once, in high school, I took Eddie Shawgo winter fly fishing in my father's new pickup. Eddie and I had planned to float Blue Duns on a river not too far from home, but as we were driving in, the vehicle executed a series of heart-stopping 360s, slid off the pavement, and buried itself near where a little spring creek poured through a culvert. Without even trying to restart the truck, I took my fly rod from the gun rack behind the seat. "Let's fish here," I said, and we did.

Yes, there was a time in my life when my primary consideration was finding fish, and getting to a stream or lake was a lot more important than getting home again. Lately, however, the polar ice caps have moved down, the Earth's crust has become unstable, and the government has been messing so much with the metric system that they've lengthened the mile. As a result, late afternoons on the water are much cooler than they used to be, and when I finally head back to the car, it's twice as far away as it was when I parked it. I'm tired, I'm cold, and I'm usually hungry; I want to go home. It has therefore become very important that I carefully map the trip back to my four-wheeled sanctuary to avoid plowed fields, cedar swamps, and railroad tracks.

Sometimes, even on public land, devious landowners rush out when they hear I am in the area and turn up all the acreage between my vehicle and me. It is a formidable task to navigate just-plowed fields in waders. Put a little rain on those fields, and the task becomes torturous. When you try to walk across this gumbo it attaches itself to the bottoms of your boots. Fly fishers with a fear of heights should be especially wary of wet, plowed fields, as the accumulation of mud on cleated soles can increase your distance from the ground by several feet. Of course, this does make the vehicle easier to spot and seem tantalizingly close, but it slows considerably the process of getting to it.

Unless you're into terror and self-disfigurement, cedar swamps should also be avoided on the way back to your vehicle. They are dark and musty, with deadfalls for your shins and flushing grouse for your heart. There is quicksand. There are stinging plants, and mosquitoes so big they are as likely to carry you home as devour you on the spot. When you are already dead tired and sucking in spider webs as you fight a herd of charley horses, you are in no condition to engage in mortal combat with an insect.

Railroad tracks are the worst day-end walking there is. Deceptively uneven, they cannot be walked without jarring your vertebrae, and the ties are placed just the right distance apart to discourage dignity in hip boots. Lengthen your step to skip the middle tie and you pull groin muscles; shorten them and your gait resembles that of a geisha girl with bunions. Either way, your ETA is set back a minimum of two hours. This is particularly discouraging when the car is in view the entire time.

My favorite day-end hikes? I like mossy logging roads, well-used deer trails, and grassy meadows. Add any of the unsanitary members of the bovine persuasion, however, and I'll take railroad tracks through a cedar swamp every time.

A Most Delightful Discombobulation

◆

B lowing a shot at a wide-racked whitetail as it skulks across a forest clearing is a gunning tradition, but personally I reserve special affection for those who become discombobulated while fly fishing. There is something special about the man who becomes agitated at the rise of a mere fish, an endearing quality about a guy who can miss the strike and dislocate his wrist at the same time. The smaller the fish, in fact, the more intense my feeling.

I once fished side by side with an elderly gentleman on New Mexico's San Juan River and liked the man so much I tried to line him up with my 25-year-old sister. The old boy had been fishing for trout all over the world for most of his 81 years, and he still became absolutely weak-kneed when even a small one swirled at his size-6 grasshopper imitation. A 10-pound rainbow can excite anyone, but the man who loses his composure over a 12-ouncer is my kind of people.

Actually, shaking knees and blown casts are nothing to me. When I first began fly fishing, I was inclined toward more bizarre forms of fishing fever. On my initial trip at age 12, I treated my older cousin Dewey to an exhibition I have never since been able to live down.

It was 1956—opening day of trout season, and at first light Dewey had me at the head of a wide, deep pool on a clear feeder creek.

"The first one is yours," Dewey said as he indicated a Volkswagen-size boulder near the right bank. "Drop the fly upstream on the left side and let it wash into the darker water."

I had been practicing for this moment in the backyard for three months, and I don't remember thinking about whether my cast was good or bad. When the 13-inch rainbow hurled himself skyward, I dropped the rod and flopped to my belly. One moment I was poised and alert, and the next I was face down in the shallows. From far off, it seemed, I could hear Dewey's voice.

"Why didn't you set the hook?" he whined.

I thought it odd he didn't ask about the wet sand clogging my nostrils. "I'm not sure," I answered. "It wasn't like what I had imagined." I searched his face for an indication that perhaps similar belly flops were common to other first-timers, but his arched eyebrows revealed only disbelief in the spectacle he had witnessed.

On my next opportunity at a rising trout, I stood transfixed and watched until at last it quit feeding. Then I took off, sloshing through the pool, wielding my landing net overhead like a club. "These ain't butterflies," Dewey said dryly when I returned to shore. "You sure are fun to watch, though."

Although I took no fish that day, I did practice all the basic mistakes, even managing to lasso Dewey a time or two. He was particularly in awe of the time I set the hook, missed, and smacked myself in the face. This resulted in my longest nosebleed ever.

It has been 45 years since that first fly-fishing trip. I've mellowed some and my casting has improved some, but I still go weak in the knees when a trout rises in a still pool. You may see me sometime—a tall, 50-ish man with a white beard and bald dome, talking to himself and missing more strikes than he should. You needn't sympathize, though; if this slightly abnormal behavior ever diminishes, I'll sell my 4-weight and relinquish mind and body to the boob tube. Then you can feel sorry for me.

My Great Infidelity

❖

My "Great Infidelity" began innocently enough during the summer of '83. Armed with a garden hose, I was attempting to hold off the battalion of grasshoppers advancing on my roses when my son pedaled into the yard carrying a huge rainbow strung to the handlebars of his bike. "Hey," he yelled, when he saw the objects of my hostility, "you're killin' my bait. Go mess with an aphid or somethin'!"

At 12, Matthew was still a bait fisherman. Not yet able to experience fulfillment without fillets, he kept nearly everything he caught. Several nice fish had already appeared ingloriously thus in our backyard, but my eyes nearly popped from my head when I saw this one—5 pounds if it was an ounce. I'd never caught a 5-pound trout in my life.

That evening, my son took me happily to his secret spot, and as I cast my hopper imitations, he drifted the real thing. By nightfall, he had two rainbows, each more than a pound. I had nothing.

The next evening, with no little guilt, I hid my fly vest and 5-weight in the guest closet. After years as a fly fisher, I didn't want my precious Payne to witness the regression about to begin. Then Matt and I went out again, and we both caught fish on a live grasshopper. After that, cheating became too easy.

But there was a problem. During the whole time I was skewering grasshoppers, I depended on Matthew to supply our needs. Then he went off to camp for two weeks, leaving me hopperless. Alone, I wandered into the vacant lot next door to gather my bait, but an hour later my jar was still empty. Catching fish with Matthew's hoppers had been easy; catching hoppers without Matthew was not. It seemed I would have to forsake more than my fly vest and rod to become a bait fisherman; I would also have to give up other adult peculiarities—things like cosmopolitan cool, intolerance for tedium, and caring whether the neighbors thought me a simpleton. So be it. In frustration, I armed myself with a broom and began to flail at the weeds.

"Hey, neighbor!" Herb hollered from across the fence. "When you're done beatin' the dust out of that field, come on over and I'll buy you a straitjacket."

Ignoring his sarcastic taunts, I plowed red-faced through the weeds, frantically swatting at everything that moved—"stunning them," I called it. In 40 minutes, I stunned eight grasshoppers, three spiders, and two pocket gophers. The pocket gophers recovered, but when I finally got to the creek, the grasshoppers were not showing similar inclinations. "Permanently stunning them," I called it.

Narrow, deep, and difficult to access, Dragoon Creek was the epitome of "fishiness." Even with "permanently stunned" bait, I soon landed one 12-inch rainbow and lost its twin. Then, beside a particularly dark pool, I flipped another grasshopper into the foam and immediately set the hook into a magnificent fish.

Surging, rolling, shaking his head, the trout did all those wonderful fishy things before I led him into the shallows. But the whole time, I could not chase a recurring thought: wouldn't this be fun on a dry fly? Wouldn't this be something?

The infidelity had run its course; my brief fling was over. In a few years Matthew would grow enough to try fly fishing. Then he'd be releasing fish too. Shouldn't I be waiting to show him the way? I grinned sheepishly at the thought of my Payne standing there in the guest closet. I now knew a pool where a 7-pound rainbow lived, and the knowledge that my son might take him someday on a dry fly made me infinitely happy.

Listen Up, Son

❦

O K, Son, listen up; it would be best if we didn't have to discuss this again. You tell me you've finally found the one, the perfect mate, the ultimate companion for a long-term relationship. You extol the bounteous virtues of your newest "Miss Wonderful," mentioning her looks, her figure, her intelligence, and her athleticism. Nothing wrong with that, though I'd be a lot more impressed had you also included things like common sense, a sense of humor, a fondness for dogs, and a basic understanding of the two-handed double-haul cast.

But the kicker, my boy—the thing that raised the red flag for ol' Dad—was when you looked at me and smiled really happy-like and said, " . . . And she lets me go fly fishing."

Son, I thought I taught you better than that. My lad, it is no more a woman's place to "let" you go hunting or fishing or golfing than it is your place to "let" her go shopping or skiing or sky diving or spelunking. If that's what she does, that's what she does. Would you want to be responsible for giving her permission to also pursue those other things that delight her?

The fact that she loves you doesn't mean she can't have other passions. And the same goes for you. If she "lets" you go fishing, it suggests she is making a concession, and thus her permission becomes a bargaining tool. That's not healthy. For you and me and a whole bunch of other guys out there, fly fishing is a necessity— part of who we are. If you are a good person, a good mate, a good father, permission is not needed to enjoy what you enjoy.

The word "let" suggests there is a potential for jealousy, and I would be very cautious about trying to share my life and begin a family with someone who could be jealous of something that brings me so much healthy pleasure.

Again, I am not suggesting that your new love should make

concessions to any destructive or immoral tendencies you might develop. Not that you would, just because your father did, but. . . . Well, anyway, it's a commonsense thing, lad. "Drinking with the boys," philandering, and not voting are examples of destructive acts. I'm not worried, though; you have been a fisherman since you were 3, and as far as I can tell, your passion for dark pools, cane rods, and the sweet outdoors in general have molded you into an unbelievably fine young man. You have overcome some questionable genes, and I don't see that changing anytime soon.

After you and Miss Wonderful left the other night, Lacey and I sat up and talked about our own relationship. I told her how much she was appreciated and how thankful I am that we have so much in common. I told her that after talking to other men, I sometimes am overwhelmed by the fact she and I are such a perfect match.

"You appreciate a trout finning in a quiet pool more than a dress on a rack at Nordstrom," I told her. (You can see I'm quite the romantic.)

"That's because a trout finning in a quiet pool doesn't remind me of how wide my hips are," she said.

And while her comment had absolutely nothing at all to do with what I have been trying to say, Son, if you can figure out a benign yet appropriate response to her lament, you are even better husband material than I.

The Devil Craft

I get apprehensive about this time each year when the water begins to warm. Warming water means my wife and daughters will begin planning a canoe/fly-fishing/camping extravaganza, and unfortunately for this attempt at familial bonding, canoeing is the one nice-weather "outdoorsy" activity besides drowning I do not care for.

My aversion to canoes goes back to a solo fishing float in Utah many years ago. Wanting very much to prove I could do it, I set out in April in a 12-foot model to fly fish and camp the 7-mile stretch of the Green River between the spillway ramp and the take-out at Little Hole. I had planned on a leisurely two days, but three minutes into my adventure I learned something very interesting about canoes: they don't sink, even when they tip over and fill up with water. Cameras and cooking utensils, food and fly rods, on the other hand, do. Very interesting indeed.

It was quite chilly that day, but there was no turning back because my vehicle was waiting at the take-out. I forged ahead, "navigating" the Green River in 10 hours of frenzied, frozen paddling. During that time, I stopped only to right my capsized devil craft each time I moved too far to the left or the right of its delicate, unforgiving point of balance. One would think that by the time I finally reached my vehicle, I would have gained a measure of competence with a canoe paddle. One would have thought incorrectly. I vowed to never sit in another canoe.

I kept this promise for more than five years, but my summers of bug-spray abuse in Alaska evidently destroyed some brain cells and, on the advice of my cousin Dwayne, I committed to another trip. This time it was along Colorado's Fryingpan River below Ruedi Reservoir, because Dwayne had assured me it was not only loaded with rainbows, but easy to navigate in early summer. It was both, but a timid, inexperienced canoeist cannot paddle a devil craft fast enough to stay in front of horseflies; they dined on all exposed body parts the entire way. I also noted that when one has been in a canoe for so many tense miles, one does not immediately adjust to standing upright. Afterward, I got a lot of odd looks as I duckwalked into a Jiffy Mart looking for calamine lotion.

Believe it or not, I actually purchased a canoe in 1995. I did this because I suffer from "Depression Syndrome," an affliction affecting millions of Americans who either lived through the Great Depression or had parents who did. The primary symptom is an overpowering urge to buy anything on sale, even if it isn't needed. What child of the Great Depression could turn down a $400 fiber-glass canoe for $50?

Actually, after I purchased the deceitful monster, I was more than happy to just let it sit. It looked pretty good turned upside down beside the garage, a suggestion of youth and robust athleticism. Sadly, my wife and daughters thought we should "get our money out of it."

"Hey," I protest each spring, "it was only 50 bucks! I get 50 bucks' worth of enjoyment just throwing a rock at it now and then."

Of course, that doesn't wash. That's why, any day now, we will be packing for our annual fishing/camping float. This year, my sympathetic son has sent me a waterproof duffel bag for my camera, wallet, and lunch. What I'd like to have is a larger one I can put my whole body in.

The Drift Boat

❖❖❖

Last summer, Mike Sweeney and I took our drift boat fantasies to the next level and bought a 12-foot wooden fixer-upper with a heavy-duty if homely trailer. The first couple of days after we brought her home, we did a little sanding, bought some sealer, and spent several evenings talking about how great it was going to be this winter on the Snake River, away from the hoards of steelhead fishermen on the Grande Ronde. We spent a lot of time just admiring our purchase, kicking the trailer tires, and taking a few measurements. In our zeal to possess a fly-fishing getaway vessel, we had disregarded a very important shared deficiency: together we are as dexterous as a soup bone. Mike is the kind of guy who hurts himself with sandpaper. I'm the kind of guy who admires Mike's ability to call the doctor without strangling himself on the phone cord. If Mike and I were ever going to use the boat, we'd need help.

Over the next two weeks, a half dozen or so people appeared at odd hours in our driveway, but my wife said very little until the afternoon she found Herb Groshoff lying in her nasturtiums as he repacked the bearings on the boat trailer.

"Alan," she hissed as I bent over Herb, offering small talk and encouragement, "why is that man smashing my nasturtiums?"

"Because they're in his way?" I offered hopefully.

Lacey closed her eyes and exhaled sharply—making the sound a prizefighter makes when he takes a solid jab in the chest. "Wrong answer, dear," she said. "That's what you said last week, when Jack Wood leveled my petunias."

"Jack was patching a hole in the bow, sweetheart," I said. "A very important favor. I didn't want to get all cranky about a few petunias."

Lacey looked out over the violated vegetation lining the driveway and slowly shook her head. "These boat people of yours are destroying my flowers," she said. "Why are they spending so much time on that goofy-looking boat?"

"Because we had to make them partners to get the work done," I told her.

Lacey screwed up her face and glanced back again to where Herb was thrashing about in the orange flowers, a boot heel up-rooting another clump of blooms. "So," she said at last, "you four are partners, huh?"

"And Bob Aho, too," I admitted. "He's going to refinish the seats. You remember Bob—the lilac bush?"

"Oh yes—the rare French double. I could never forget Bob."

"Yeah, Bob won't forget you, either, Lacey. You never should have said that about his mother. He's very proud of his heritage."

Lacey shook her head demurely. "So, it's you and Mike and Jack and Herb and Bob, then?"

"And Thayer and his Uncle Dwayne. And Steve and Rod and Rod's cousin. They're all helping."

Lacey was shaking her head. "That's 10 people, including yourself. You don't have a partnership," she said, "you have a corporation. I thought you and Mike wanted to get away from the crowds."

"Yeah, we've been thinking about that lately, too," I said. "So this morning we donated our interest in this fine craft to Herb and Jack and Bob and Thayer and Dwayne and Steve and Rod and Rod's cousin. As soon as they get finished, they'll all be out on the Snake, and Mike and I will have the Grande Ronde to ourselves."

Just in Case

❖

Ido know I'm mortal, but making out a will has always seemed to me a morbid concession to this mortality; I don't like the idea in the least. And while I also believe in a Greater Being, I am not particularly keen on joining Him just yet. It has not been proven to my satisfaction that there are dark trout pools, misty mountain lakes, and quiet beaver ponds in heaven. I hope that one day someone will ease my mind of these concerns, for, having been a fisherman for all but about the first four years of my life, sitting on a cloud with a harp is not my idea of a perfect way to spend leisure time.

I have read that members of ancient civilizations had their favorite wives, horses, and foods buried with them to make their journey through the afterworld more comfortable. This raises the hope that the old boys knew something I do not. I would feel ever so much better if I could not only take my 4-weight bamboo rod with me, but know I would get a chance to use it once I was settled.

There is something about a bamboo fly rod, and I value mine above all other angling possessions. The rest of my fishin' stuff is just that—possessions lumped in a broad, disorganized category and consigned to the basement or storage shed.

Though I have owned but four, bamboo rods please me. They're nice to look at. My love for them is rooted not so much in tradition as in the unshakable feeling that with any other rod I would miss more takes and have less fun. When I'm on the water, my bamboo fly rod is an appendage rather than an extension, and I feel good that it is attached.

My first bamboo was a South Bend sadly in need of refinishing. I inherited it from my father, who had bought it used for $20. It was a low-end rod to begin with, a club by today's standards. It had a nasty habit of becoming disjointed at critical moments, an affliction that created considerable confusion and generated quite a few stares when it was time to net a really big rainbow. Nevertheless, we netted a bunch.

My next bamboo rod was a Shakespeare of slightly better quality. I purchased it after the South Bend had its final, lethal encounter with the back screen door. The Shakespeare, too, was well used, and I quickly discovered why it had been offered so cheaply at a garage sale: you couldn't keep a reel attached for anything. Until I gave up and started using friction tape, I spent a fair number of hours feeling around underwater, searching for my old Hardy. This was not an ideal situation.

One of my most vivid early fly-fishing memories is of hanging by my ankles in the grasp of my friend Mike Sweeney, groping under the waters of the Big Spokane River for a reel that had fallen off as I began to string my line. The memory is fortified by the fact that it was December, 8 degrees below zero, and the city still dumped untreated sewage into the river. Miraculously, I recovered the reel, and it wasn't long after I got out of the hospital that I put it on a new 7-weight Leonard.

Today I mostly use a 7-foot 6-inch, 4-weight Orvis because I'm older, it's lighter, and I have been led to believe that because one's finesse improves with age, a 4-weight is all I need. Like its predecessors, it is comfortable in my hand, and when I do finally buy the farm, I'm sure my heirs will forgive me for not making it part of my estate. Yes, I have drawn up a will, and my Orvis is to go with me. Just in case. Maybe it's wasteful, but you just don't want to take chances with important stuff like that.

Usually

❦

When you are a child, the word you least like to hear is "no." Most likely, it is pronounced emphatically— "NO!"—and you are fairly certain you will die because you have been denied an important life experience—like cutting your brother's hair or putting Silly Putty in the microwave.

When you get to be a little bigger, you learn to despise the word "maybe" almost as much as "no." "Maybe" is essentially the same as "no," but with a false glimmer of hope. "Maybe" is used mostly by parents who don't want to deal with the whimpering, whining, or obligatory explanations that accompany "NO!"

When you are mature, as I am supposed to be, you eventually develop a dread for "usually." It seems like such an innocent word, but in certain instances it can ruin a perfectly good day:

Usually, a cough like that goes away in a few days.

Usually, Drano will fix that.

Usually, a rattle like that is just a pebble under the hubcap.

Usually, this car has enough gas for 20 more miles once the "check engine" light comes on.

Usually, you never see a state patrolman on this section of highway.

Usually, that dog wouldn't harm a flea.

Usually, we can fix something like that for under $500.

Usually, a mosquito bite like that just itches a little.

Usually, your child is fairly well behaved.

In romantic endeavors and dating, the word "usually," if not downright crushing, is at least ego deflating:

Usually, I don't have problems following a man's lead.

Usually, I find a man with a beard to be sexy.

Usually, you can hardly see these boils.

Usually, I never fall asleep at dinner.

Usually, I'm able to find a baby-sitter.

When you spend a considerable portion of your life fly fishing and engaging in all of the outdoor activities that go with it—like camping, hiking, wading, float tubing, and eating beans out of a can, "usually" is particularly bad. Fly fishermen are naturally optimistic. We venture forth knowing there is more to our passion than the fish at the end of the line, but are nevertheless hopeful the day will offer more than a suntan or a knee-wrenching wade over slick river boulders. "Usually" is a sure sign things aren't going as well as you had hoped they would:

Usually, you can stand in this current.

Usually, a graphite is pretty tough to break.

Usually, this tent doesn't leak.

Usually, I remember the can opener.

Usually, the mosquitoes are gone by this time of year.

Usually, no one gets sick drinking from this stream.

Usually, it's pretty quiet here.

Usually, we have a fish by now.

Usually, the water isn't so high . . . or low . . . or muddy . . . or cold.

Usually, the beavers here are pretty docile.

Usually, this stove will fire right up.

Usually, there's no one else fishing this pool.

Usually, my dog sits pretty still in a canoe.

Usually, those belly-boats can take more abuse than that.

Usually, I bring a second reel for emergencies like this.

Usually, you can get a barbless hook out of your eyebrow a lot easier than that.

Usually, my mother-in-law doesn't want to come along on trips like this.

I can count on the fingers of one hand my fishing days without a "usually," but life is a dance, and I guess the little missteps make it interesting, even invigorating. "Usually" flushes ugly cholesterol and at the same time reminds you that pandemonium is not the norm. "Usually" makes you feel alive. Usually.

Howard's Hell-Hole

I have this hypothesis I inherited during my ninth year when my Aunt Judy had me spade her rock-hard garden.

"Sonny," she said as I wiped off perspiration and tried to straighten my cramping lower back, "anything worth anything is worth suffering for."

Aunt Judy assured me I would appreciate the watermelons we were going to grow twice as much when I considered the work I had done. I believed her, too, but later that summer, when those "watermelons" turned to Brussels sprouts, I quit hanging around her place. I sure as heck would not have spent all those miserable hours with a spade had I known she was planting poisonous vegetables.

Despite the deception, Aunt Judy's theory about suffering stayed with me, helping to smooth the perilous path through numerous childhood and adolescent traumas. Now that I am an adult, I figure the least I can do for assorted nieces and nephews is teach them what I learned by taking them to Howard's Hell-Hole.

Why old man Howard decided to build a cabin way back behind Blue Swamp, no one knows for sure. Why he thought his bride, Flossie Dee, would want to live there is an even greater puzzlement. The facts are, though, he did and she didn't, and when she left him to pursue the American Dream with a tenacious brush salesman, Mr. Howard chalked it up to either bad luck or great brushes and stayed on. Eventually, his truck broke down, and the narrow path he had cut through the wilderness became overgrown with willows and alders and all sorts of stinging, grabbing things.

On weekends during the springs and summers of my high school years I would plow through this jungle in my father's truck, park by the wooden bridge, then muck a few hundred yards through a dense cedar swamp. There, a beaver dam had backed up the water, forming an acre-size pond loaded with brook trout.

Sometimes, Mr. Howard himself would be there, but he never seemed to mind my intrusion. "Ain't my fish," he told me when I asked if I could share the water.

After high school I went off to college, and the alders and willows on Mr. Howard's road used those years to grow thicker and unyielding. By the time I had graduated and come home, taking a vehicle within two miles of the old pond was out of the question. Still, the memory of those fat brook trout wouldn't let me sleep, and before long I walked in from the highway.

Actually, "walked" is inaccurate. Mr. Howard's path through the wilderness had become a nearly impenetrable tangle. I sloshed, I crawled, I clawed, and I cursed. I lost a boot and snapped the tip off a new fly rod. Devil's club reached out to raise welts, and diabolical tree roots snared my feet, holding me captive for voracious mosquitoes. When I finally reached Howard's cabin, I found it sagging and deserted, but the brookies were still there in the pond among the trees, and they attacked my fly with abandon.

Today, I use Howard's Hell-Hole for my own enrichment, but I also use it as a barometer of promise for assorted nieces and nephews. If Jake or Emily or little Derrick wants to do something "outdoorsy" with Uncle Alan merely because the TV isn't working, that isn't good enough. If they really want to experience fly fishing, though, they can come stand beside me on a beaver dam at dawn and watch fingers of mist wind like cotton candy among the cedar. First, though, they've got to get there. If they ask to go again, they've got what it takes.

Entitlements

◆

I probably would have never considered cleaning my side of the closet had I been able to find my favorite fishing hat. It wasn't in its usual place on the floor behind the washroom door, however, and Mike Sweeney was picking me up in 15 minutes for another go at those East River browns.

When Lacey and I built this place we put a walk-in closet in the master bedroom with a rack and shelf for me on the south wall and one for her on the north. Although I doubted I had hung the hat where it belonged, I figured there was a pretty good chance it was somewhere in the house. As luck would have it, Lacey was in the closet sorting through a basketful of shoes.

"So this is where you've been hiding all morning," I said. "I thought you'd gone to town for plumbing supplies."

Lacey rolled her eyes and gave me THAT LOOK—the one that originated when Noah came home one afternoon and explained to his spouse that he was going to build a really big fishing boat. It has been refined by wives ever since. "Alan," she said, "I told you 20 minutes ago I was going up to reorganize the closet."

I shrugged. "I thought you said, 'Replace the faucet.' Reorganizing the closet should be a lot cheaper. Say, have you seen my fishing hat—the one with the Western Green Drake embedded in the bill?"

"Is it my week to watch it?" Lacey stood up and tossed a pair of shoes out the closet door and into a cardboard box.

"Hey," I said, "Those are my new wingtips."

"Well, you've got part of that right," Lacey replied.

"Those are wingtips. They have been here without being worn since your father passed away four years ago."

"Dad liked those shoes," I said.

"Yes, but you don't, Alan. That doesn't make you a bad son. I'm giving them to Goodwill."

"My life? My legacy? You're giving my legacy to Goodwill?"

Lacey found a pair of low-cut black Converse tennis shoes, circa 1962, and tossed them into the box also. "I'm chucking the leisure suits too, Mr. Disco King," she told me. "Alan—this stuff is ancient!"

I dove into the cardboard box, retrieving the tennis shoes. "Lacey," I said, "what gives you the right to come up here and start throwing out my fishin' stuff? I wear these shoes when I fish Sand Creek! I never in a million years would consider cleaning out your side of the closet."

"You wouldn't need to," Lacey responded. "I don't keep junk. Besides," she added, "throwing out a husband's old clothes is a God-given female entitlement. It's one of the benefits of my femininity."

"Like the reason you get to take bubble baths and I don't? Or the fact you can stay home alone reading trashy novels without being judged sexually dysfunctional and I can't?"

"Something like that."

"And tell me, dear," I said. "What 'entitlements' do I have as a member in good standing of the male species?"

Lacey didn't hesitate. "You have the right to make loud, obnoxious, socially unacceptable noises in public," she said. "You have the right to fall asleep on the carpet after Thanksgiving dinner, to whine loudly when you get the sniffles, to have intimate conversations with other males about 'double hauls' and 'matching hatches.' You have the right to . . ."

"OK, OK," I said, extending both palms in resignation. "So I get all that, and you get to toss my old clothes?"

"Essentially."

I smiled as I backed out of the closet. It sounded like a good deal to me.

Fear Is a Wonderful Thing

❖

According to everything I had read, one didn't need a boat to enjoy British Columbia's fishing. This was good, for I didn't have one. What I did have, 20 years ago, was some time, so at age 35 I set off on a three-month shoestring adventure with the goal of catching five species of salmon, as well as pike, grayling, and lake trout, on a fly.

By the time I got to far northern B.C., I was still minus a laker, and to take one, it was obvious I needed to get out on some big water. At a café in the town of Dease Lake, I made some inquiries, and the sympathetic cook took an interest.

"No money, huh?" he said. "Got anything to trade?"

An hour later, I stood in his garage while he climbed over a mountain of accumulated treasures looking for his vinyl two-man raft. Finally, he reached in among the moose antlers and toboggans and came up holding a patched, amorphous, blue and yellow mass.

"She's yours for a tire and rim," he said. "The paddle is free."

To be honest, I wasn't thrilled at the prospect of completing my trip without a spare tire, but the prospect of taking a laker on a fly—perhaps even a large laker—short-circuited my common sense. The next morning I took my craft to Dease Lake and proceeded to inflate it.

A half hour later, the heap of vinyl had assumed only a vague likeness of a two-man boat, and I lay on the ground beside it hyperventilating. My eyes bulged, my ears were popping, and the muscles in my face had stretched so far my lips looked rather like those of a sturgeon. Evidently, a two-man raft needed two men to inflate it, and both needed the lung capacity of a Sherpa. I could have blown up the Goodyear blimp with less effort.

Luckily, a friendly bicyclist pulled into the launch area and offered to call a doctor. Instead, I talked him into loaning me his tire pump. In 10 minutes my raft was plump with air, and after carefully tucking my lips into my mouth, where they wouldn't be in my way, I was off.

Stroking steadily, I cruised to midlake and began casting with a sinking-tip line and a large Mylar-dressed fly. For the next hundred yards, I paddled and cast, paddled and cast. When I decided at last to move farther down the lake, my boat seemed sluggish and I noticed I was riding much lower in the water than what seemed safe. While I searched my brain for a fragment of forgotten physics to explain these developments, the first cold stream of water trickled over the side. It had, I quickly decided, something to do with sinking.

Fear is a wonderful thing; it enables one to surmount the insurmountable. At the rate I was losing air, there was no way I could simultaneously reinflate that raft by mouth while paddling for shore. But I did. Before I reached the beach, in fact, my vessel had more air in it than when I had begun, and I had created a rooster tail that carried me 20 feet onto dry land.

I hadn't caught my lake trout on a fly, but somehow it didn't seem to matter. I kissed terra firma, leaned back, and inhaled deeply. Lake trout weren't nearly as important as blowing out the candles on my next birthday cake. And I sure had the lips for that now.

The Slide Show

❧

Now, isn't this something? The whole family together for Thanksgiving dinner. How many years has it been, Uncle Pat? Six or seven? Right after you caught that 12-pound brown in Chimikain Creek. On a size-14 nymph, wasn't it?

Oops, sorry, Aunt Molly—I forgot we weren't going to talk about it anymore. Yes, I agree that you probably got your fill of that story. . . . Uncle Pat, why don't you just put the snapshots back in your wallet for now? Yes, the 8-by-10, too. Just slide your chair around and watch the screen—we'll clear the table later.

Aunt Molly, you can take my recliner. I've got quite a few slides here, and you'll want to be comfort— NOT YET! . . . No, no, don't feel bad, Aunt Molly, that yellow cat was a nuisance. Jennifer— help your great-aunt find her dentures. I think they flopped up there in the fruit salad. Lacey, if you'll get the lights, Matthew will run the projector and . . . Matthew! Grab your Aunt Sally! . . . Whaddaya mean, you're leaving, Aunt Sally? You're going to love this. Jennifer—bring Aunt Sally another shot of that huckleberry wine. Cousin Georgie—you stand by the door and make sure no one tries to sneak out. Matthew—slide please.

Now, this is lovely—the entrance to Holy Family Hospital in August. Just look at the petunias! That's me on the stretcher by the front door. Broken ankle—Crab Creek. Caught two nice rainbows that day, but man-oh-man are those rocks ever slippery! Matthew— slide, please.

Here we have Mike Sweeney teaching Lacey how to do a roll cast. Can you see that size-12 Great Speckled Olive Dun in Mike's right ear? No, Rachel, that is not what Mike taught her to do, but I personally think it was worth it. He made at least two spectacular runs and a dazzling leap before he broke off. Slide, please.

As you can see, this is Holy Family Hospital again. As you can also see, the petunias are dead. That's because it's winter. That's still me on the stretcher, though—Crab Creek again. This was probably my most embarrassing day afield ever. . . . Yes, Aunt Molly, that is a tree branch sticking out from beneath the blanket. . . . Never mind where it stuck me, Cousin Bob—it stuck me, OK? Slide, please, Matthew.

Isn't this pretty? Dragoon Creek in late March. That's Mike again, fishing a stonefly imitation below Riley's Bend. . . . Well, of course you can't see him, Uncle Pat—he's underwater. See those little bubbles just to the right of the big rock? That's Mike. Dragoon is a lot swifter in March than it is in May. Slide, please.

I'm amazed the Reverend Jack's camera was still working for this shot. That's the bottom of my canoe you see there in the Palouse River. I'm under it. The Palouse is a pretty decent smallmouth water in the early spring—big crawdad imitations. Lots of snags, though. . . . Yes, Bonnie Rae, we usually sit in the canoe, but your Uncle Alan was being silly. . . . No, Sally, Jack doesn't fish with me anymore. Not from a canoe, anyway. Slide, please.

Here's Dad's second cousin's kid, Newton, at his high school graduation. None of us thought Newton would ever get out of kindergar— Hey! What's this doing here? Give me the next one, Matthew.

Cousin Yolanda's wedding? Lacey! Get the lights! Someone's been messing with my slides. HEY! Where is everyone, Matthew? . . . In the kitchen? . . . Mincemeat pie? . . . Pumpkin, too? Oh, I suppose I could eat a couple of pieces. Get the lights, kid. And a napkin. We can watch these slides anytime.

All About Money

❖

Whaen I got my first morning paper route, my father would occasionally help me deliver the heavy Sunday edition so we could go fishing afterwards. We would walk down to the corner together in the dark and wait for the truck, watching lights flick on as the city yawned and awakened. Mostly, we talked about school and baseball and dry flies, and I grew up knowing there was a right way and a wrong way in anything.

Dad explained the world of finance to me during these walks in three simple steps:

1. "If you can't afford it, don't buy it."
2. "If you have a debt, pay it."
3. "You get ahead in the world by working hard and saving."

Dad's philosophy has served me well, but conflicts terribly with the second-millennium mentality that goes more like this:

1. "If you can't afford it, put it on your charge card."
2. "If you have a debt, file for bankruptcy."
3. "You get ahead in the world when your father-in-law buys the company or your stocks split."

Mostly, I have followed my father's conservative financial advice, which includes picking up pennies. Kids today won't even bend over to pick up a penny. When I was a kid, your own father would run over you trying to claim that single piece of copper gleaming on the sidewalk. I'm not rich, but I'm not wanting, either—except maybe for another 3-weight, a fly-fishing vacation for peacock bass on the Amazon River, and a float tube that doesn't need periodic midlake inflation. Once in awhile, I will use my charge card, but only for the sake of convenience, as in "Putting this new Loomis on The Card, darling, will be a lot more convenient than robbing a bank to pay cash."

I read in the paper that credit card companies are considering dropping customers who pay off their balances each month because the companies can't make any money that way. I do not understand, then, why, when my payment is late—something that happens about once a year—the nice charge card people send me a friendly letter that goes something like this:

Dear Deadbeat Loser:

You won't get away with it. If we do not receive your minimum payment in three days, you will be hearing from Bennie the Torch. We know where you live.

XXX 000,

The Friendly Folks Downtown

P.S. If this letter and your payment have crossed in the mail, please disregard the above and try to get a good night's sleep.

If credit card companies had reasonable billing dates, I wouldn't get letters like this ever. Credit card bills are sent on the 15th day of one month and are due on the 2nd of the next. Though I like to pay my bills promptly, I get my own check on the last day of the month. I can't pay a bill on the 15th because I am already broke, and a bill paid on the last day of one month has no time to go anywhere by the second day of the next month.

Lacey says I could compensate for all this by making out a check on the 15th, stashing it somewhere, and then mailing it out on, say, the 27th or 28th. She forgets she is talking to a man who can't keep track of the soap in the shower and sometimes forgets to put wading boots on over his socks.

My Poor, Dear Mother

———— ❧ ————

My dad and I used to take long summer fly-fishing vacations to the blue-ribbon streams in Montana, Colorado, and even Utah and New Mexico. I loved it when it was just the two of us, but sometimes Mom came too. Things got complicated then.

When my father decided he'd had enough driving for the day, he would say, "What do you think, Mother? Should we get a motel with a pool?"

At that, my heart would jump. A motel with a pool was a really big deal to a kid who had been sitting all day in the back seat of a '49 Ford, staring at heat waves and counting smashed jackrabbits.

"That would be nice," Mom would say. "I'll keep my eye out."

For blocks and blocks and blocks, then, Mom would keep her eye out until finally . . . "There's one," she'd say. "The sign says it's $6.50—with a kitchenette . . ."

Bonanza! I'd start shedding my shoes and socks even as we pulled in.

". . . but I'll have to look at it first," Mom would add.

My mother would then go into the motel office, and pretty soon she'd come back out with the manager and the two of them would disappear into one of the look-alike lower units.

"The toilet is dirty," she'd say when she came back to the car, and without a word Dad would start up the stifling-hot Ford and pull back onto the highway.

It would have done no good for me to tell Mom I didn't mind a dirty toilet. If I couldn't be fishing I needed to be swimming, and when it came to a motel with a swimming pool, I didn't mind if there were alligators in the toilet and black mambas under the bed. We'd just keep driving until at last Mom found a place without a pool where the toilets met her standards.

I thought about my mother's elaborate motel routine several times this past February as Lacey and I were fishing our way to New Mexico to sample the trout on the San Juan River. My usual method for selecting a motel had been to pull up to the office, go inside, pay, and take what was offered. It served us fairly well until we got to Winslow, Arizona.

Because Lacey had commented negatively about my last choice, I suggested she pick our Winslow lodging, so eventually she directed me into the gravel parking lot of an L-shaped motel.

Lacey went inside, and pretty soon a tall, gaunt man with a ponytail, a tattoo, and a large crescent wrench walked past our car and into unit 6. "He's turning on the heat," Lacey explained as she came back to the car.

When we gathered our suitcases and went to the door, the man was fiddling with the TV. "Turn on this here light switch to make the TV work," he explained gruffly. "If the toilet backs up, there's a plunger under the sink."

When he closed the door, amber light diffused through the dirt-encrusted windows, catching the cobwebs on the ceiling. The bedspread on the sagging double bed was ragged and stained— almost shiny—and a wet dog smell permeated the matted, blue shag carpet.

"I can't sleep in that bed," I told my wife.

Lacey was already sobbing. "We have to stay here!" she said. "It's paid for!"

"It doesn't matter," I said. "We'll get another one down the road." I was chuckling.

"Are you laughing at me?" Lacey asked, wiping away a tear.

"No, dear," I said. "I was just thinking about my poor, dear mother. She used to make me so mad."

Br-r-r-ring It On!

❖

When I was a very young man, I spent a good part of one winter with a 12-gauge shotgun lying under a white bedsheet in the snow. I was hoping to trick a Canada goose into landing on me, or at least nearby, and during those long, lonely vigils, I was sure I was as cold as I would ever get. Then I tried winter fly fishing in Montana, an activity wherein participants might consider lying under a sheet in the snow in order to warm up.

Though fly fishing can be excellent in the winter months, the primary goal of cold-weather fly anglers is not so much to catch fish as to avoid going home with important appendages turning black. Freezing your "num-nums," in fact, is a condition to be avoided at all costs. During the numerous Decembers of my life, I have frozen my num-nums only once, and once, I can tell you, is more than adequate. Much better to purchase, develop, or refine heat-conserving devices such as the dork hat, the liquid-fuel body igniter, and the munchkin suit.

The dork hat is essentially a wool-lined cap with earflaps that fasten beneath the chin with Velcro. If the lining is rabbit fur rather than wool or artificial fibers, and a bold dressing of this fur adorns the front, it is commonly referred to as a "mad bomber's hat." There is a certain dashing, devil-may-care look to the mad bomber's hat, a connection, I suppose, to the early days of aerial warfare. If this connection isn't important to you, it is cheaper and easier to acquire the dorkier version that makes you look as if you'd take out your brain and play with it if only you had one. No matter. The dork hat keeps you warm, and keeping warm is the name of the winter fishing game.

The liquid-fuel body igniter is really just a hand warmer that doesn't work right. I've tried the solid-fuel variety with the little sticks you can burn from both ends if it's really cold, but I don't like the way they smell. With the liquid-fuel warmers, there is always the possibility you will disappear at midstream with a mighty "WHOOSH," but when they are working they seem to give off more heat. Perhaps too much heat. My friend Antoine Purcell used to carry one in every pocket, but his wife was always complaining about the scorched underwear, and during one spectacular meltdown Antoine decided broiling his num-nums in a munchkin suit wasn't much better than freezing them.

Ah, yes. The munchkin suit. Really not a suit at all. What it is, is the concept of layering taken to the ridiculous for winter fly fishing. On my feet I wear polypropylene socks beneath two pairs of medium-weight wool socks. It is important to put these on first, because once I am fully dressed, there's no way I can bend over. Beginning with polypropylene underwear, I then don, in order, fleece pants, wool pants, coveralls, wool shirt, down vest, windbreaker, and parka. Rubber chest waders go on last. (Neoprene won't go over all the layers.) Dressed thus on a January morning, I once dropped my fly rod on the Clark Fork River, practically in downtown Missoula, and had to go completely prone to pick it up. Once the rod was in hand, I was faced with the challenge of becoming upright again. I thrashed around in the gravel on the riverbank for a good 15 minutes, attracting a sizable crowd of people, a pair of bald eagles, and a group of very determined paramedics who were certain I was having a seizure. It was extremely embarrassing.

Still, I guess it made as much sense as lying under a sheet in the snow. And at least I was warm.

These Last Days of Winter

E very year about this time I am confronted with that vener-
able late-winter question peculiar to all who fish with a fly:
What is there to do? This winter was particularly bad, as a
silly midlife crisis somehow led to a pickup basketball game at the
Y, followed by an ambulance ride to the hospital and a thigh-high
cast that won't come off for another two weeks.

For the past few months I have pretty much been stuck in the
house, and, unbelievably, Lacey and I are showing signs of irrita-
bility; I need to get out and fish, and she just needs me to get out. I
have heard cabin fever described as a 20-foot stare in a 12-foot room,
but my wife and I have reduced that room dimension by half. Even
should I be fortunate enough to avoid a direct hit, I know it is but a
matter of time before I'm leveled by a ricocheting glare. To relieve
the tension, I recently suggested that Lacey walk over to her aunt's
house. She reminded me that her aunt lives 1,500 miles from here and
then suggested I attempt a gravity-defying biological function.

This situation very much reminds me of the winter of '76, when
old Sam Peterson built a brick wall through the middle of his living
room because, as he put it, "the wife was blinking too loud." Sam
was OK again come ice-off in April, but by then the little woman
had taken off for Phoenix with the heating-oil man. I guess "spring
breakup" means different things to different folks.

Lacey has been just full of all sorts of ridiculous ideas of late to
keep me from breathing her air. Last week she suggested I go to
the basement and sharpen the kitchen knives—not a bad idea, but
we don't have a basement.

Yesterday, at her insistence, I tried to unclog the kitchen drain.
It seems I'm responsible every time the water backs up, despite the
fact that she uses the sink 10 times as frequently as I. And while
it is true I did find a couple handfuls of soggy pheasant feathers,

I don't see how she could have possibly put the blame on me, as she doesn't even allow me to wash pheasant capes in the kitchen sink. I haven't, either, except for that one time in December when she visited her sister in Sandpoint, Idaho.

Probably, had I not cracked the drainpipe in my pathetic efforts with an oversize wrench, things would be less tense around here. Just try, though, to explain to a woman with cabin fever why plumbers charge time and a half for Sunday calls.

I wonder why it is that all women assume all men are born with a mechanical bent? You'd think she'd remember the time I rewired the toaster, and every time the toast popped up, so did the garage door. That was truly my finest hour as a fixer—even better than the runaway vacuum cleaner incident that sent Lacey to the emergency room with second-degree rug burns.

Last night, Lacey was in the living room reading another book. In an attempt to make conversation, I asked her why she always chooses either mysteries or historical romances and suggested she'd perhaps be happier with one of my copies of *Wildfowl*, *Wing & Shot*, or *Northwest Fly Fishing*. She started that glaring business, so I ducked into my den and started polishing my fly vise again. I figured that as long as I'm incapacitated, I might as well do something worthwhile. Why Lacey can't find something equally constructive to pass these last days of winter is beyond me.

Fishin' Food

—◊◊—

Having recently experimented with a low-carb diet during which I subsisted on air chips and ice wraps, I was delighted to see the winter fishing season begin.

Winter fly fishing is not at all like summer fly fishing. While engaged in summer fishing, it is easy to begin feeling guilty about the number of calories being consumed between casts because the evidence of your overindulgence is pooching up over the top of your hip boots like a great, white water balloon.

Each time I take off my shirt to catch a few summer angling rays just before dropping a size-16 Yellow Sally atop a sulking Savage River rainbow, I am reminded that while Mountain Dew and potato chips are the essence of warm-weather fishing, they aren't doing much for my figure.

It's not something I dwell on, as I long ago surrendered my Mr. Universe fantasy in favor of staying within 50 pounds of my "perfect weight." Late in the summer, however, I sometimes think about the shape I'm in when I notice the sun is not tanning all parts of my belly equally. It seems to me I look rather like a tiger, with white stripes between the rolls of golden excess.

Winter fishing is much better if you view eating as part of the total experience. On a winter fishing expedition, one can get rid of all sorts of leftover holiday junk and not feel guilty about it, primarily because you don't notice its effects with all that bulky clothing on. Also, it is easier to justify overeating when the weather is cold, for who's to say when you might have to subsist on accumulated fat reserves?

My friend Mike Sweeney is my favorite person to winter fish with. Mike thinks a balanced meal is one where you have equal portions of Twinkies and potato chips. On our frequent trips, I sometimes have to remind him to "pack light" because of space limitations in the car. If this means leaving his rod, reel, and fly box at home, so be it, but Mike is never without a cooler stuffed with worthless calories: he doesn't bring candy bars; he brings candy stores. Chocolate peanut clusters, bags of M&Ms, Little Debbie Oatmeal Creme Pies—take your pick. Better yet, take lots of each. For a person like me who, as a child, could buy sweets only once a week on allowance day, Mike is The Candy Man.

Usually, I suppose as a joke, Mike's cooler also holds apples or a bag of yuppie carrots, but I suspect he recycles these. Apples do not have an "eat by" date, and when they are wrinkled and starting to turn brown, I've got a pretty good idea they are the same props I saw on the last trip.

Sometimes Mike and I never get around to catching fish. With a crackling fire heating up the landscape and the rods propped against a tree, we sometimes just sit around cultivating a sugar high, wondering what the poor folks are doing. For variety we add Cheetos or Doritos to our diet, but these are washed down with hot chocolate, and I never, ever talk about cholesterol or clogged arteries unless Mike is working on the last Krispy Kreme and I want a bite.

Soon enough, it will be spring and I'll have to shed my winter chest waders and don my light summer hip boots. Oh, Mike and I will still overindulge on grease and sugar then, but I imagine we'll sometimes feel bad about what we're doing to our bodies.

In the meantime, I'm going to pack on a few guiltless pounds. You never can tell when you'll be snowbound.

Capital Gains

◆

When he was still a teenager, my fishing buddy Samuel Connell convinced his parents and himself that fishing was an end rather than a process. A license was $5, a good Carey Special was a quarter, his cane rod and Pflueger reel had been in the family forever, and the old Chevy that delivered him to the mountains and home again got nearly 20 miles from a gallon of 29-cent regular. If he was fortunate enough to catch a good mess of fish, he figured he was bringing home some fine eating for less than a dime a pound.

Even though Sam's mother could feed the family easily on 29 cents worth of beef liver, fresh grilled brook trout eliminated ugly dinner-table scenes during which her children would gag, whine, and threaten to run away from home. Sam grew up believing his pursuit of fish was making a significant contribution to both the substance and the subsistence of the family.

During Sam's years in college, his fishing skills improved, and though the price of flies increased, his fishing expeditions were still economically sound. True, permission to fish private property was sometimes denied when Sam and five carpooling buddies rolled like circus clowns from his small vehicle onto a rancher's circular driveway, but times were different then, and more often than not a promise to close the gates and pick up their own litter was all the convincing required.

When Sam married, he could still justify his passion for fishing by appealing to his bride's economic good sense. Why eat macaroni and cheese, he asked her, when for the same price we could feast on pink trout flesh? Why spend good money on expensive recreational outlets like movies and concerts when fishing is cheaper, healthier, and more fun?

To his surprise, these arguments got Sam through an entire

season, but midway through the second, the manager of their credit union convinced Sam's wife, Maxine, that she should take charge of the checkbook. Within a week, she made a determination that Sam says changed his fishing habits forever. Your trips afield, she told him, are anything but cost effective. While it is true you are "bringing home the bacon," that "bacon" is coming to the table at $28 a pound. She said that when she factored in items like a new graphite rod, a float tube, motels, and out-of-state licenses, the figure doubled.

From that point on, Sam says, his fishing changed. No longer saddled with the responsibility of putting food on the table, no longer driven by his instinct to provide, he could fish twice as much! Like the rest of us, Sam had always anticipated the fishing season because he appreciated new country, pink sunrises, fresh air, honest exercise, and rain-washed forests. After his wife's economic revelation, he was allowed the pleasure of indulging his senses without the burden of also being productive. If a big rainbow swirled at his Adams but didn't take, Sam didn't feel like he had to make another hundred casts. If a big one broke off, he didn't need to agonize over his bad luck and tear off upstream looking for another.

One fish or none, it doesn't matter so much to Sam anymore because he releases most of them anyway. Just by being there, he says, he can go home rejuvenated, better able to face another week of commuter traffic, insensitive clerks, and a newspaper carrier who delights in seeing how far up on the roof he can put the morning edition.

Grandpapa Alan

◆◆◆◆

My son, Matt, informed me recently that I'm going to be a grandfather. I asked him how come.

"Well," Matt said, "it seems Leahlyn is pregnant."

"Pregnant!" I screamed. "You've barely been married 13 years! I turn my back on you for a few minutes and . . . what's the hurry?"

"Well," Matt said again, "Leahlyn felt her biological clock might be . . ."

"Nonsense!" I roared. "What about *my* biological clock?"

"What about your biological clock?" Matt asked.

"I'm not ready to be a grandpa!" I said. "I was just getting used to being a father. Why, lookee here—my knuckles are barely hairy and my lap isn't nearly wide enough. I can't stand gray button-down sweaters, and I still like to chase Lacey around the dining room table now and then."

"How come?" Matt asked with a grin.

"I forget," I said.

"Well, I think you're more ready to be a grandpa than you think," Matt quipped. "A young grandpa," he added. "What do you want to be called?"

"Called?"

"Yeah—what do you want your first grandchild to call you? Leahlyn was thinking maybe 'Papa Alan' or 'Grandpapa Alan' would be sort of cute."

"I think I like 'Big Al, King of the Universe,' better," I said. "Or maybe 'Most Exalted and Punctilious Nabob.'"

"That's a lot to remember," Matt said.

"Well, then, what's the matter with 'Grandpa'?" I asked. "I knew some very fine gentlemen who went by 'Grandpa.' Yours, for example. And mine, too. What's with this cutesy name thing all of a sudden? And as long as we're talking and I'm complaining, what other expectations do you have for me as a grandparent?"

"Well . . .," Matt began.

"On second thought," I interrupted, "I have some very strong thoughts of my own about grandparenting. I don't, for example, think I should feel obligated to buy any toy made of plastic—especially blue or orange plastic. Cane, more likely. Graphite at the very least. I don't think I should have to wear sweatshirts that say, 'World's Greatest Grandpa,' but I would consider 'World's Greatest Fly Fisherman.' I don't think I should be expected to keep a cupboard full of candy to bribe the little tyke when he comes to visit. And I never, ever, want him messing with my fly vise.

"I do think I should be allowed to keep the kid supplied with Lincoln Logs, books, and peacock herl, and when he gets older I'll get him a library card and a fly rod. When he gets a lot older, I'll give him a good fly rod. If he misbehaves, I'll give him a swat, and if he turns into a teenager, I'll lock him in his room."

"That sounds reasonable," Matt said. "But Leahlyn has already had an ultrasound. The doctor says we're having a girl."

"What's your point?"

"You said, 'He.' "

"Do you prefer 'It'? Boy or girl—it makes no difference to me. My expectations are the same. Little girls like Lincoln Logs and soft peacock herl, too."

"So, you don't like 'Papa Alan'?" Matt said.

"That is correct."

"And you don't plan on investing your nest egg at Toys R Us?"

"More likely The Rainbow Fly Shop."

"And there'll be some discipline mixed in with books and feathers and fishing rods and love?"

"Yup."

"Dad?"

"What?"

"That's pretty much the way you raised me."

"You can't argue with success, son," I said. "You can't argue with success."

Why I Like Liver

B elieve it or not, I'm looking forward to ice fishing. Without ice fishing, I wouldn't appreciate nymph fishing in spring and summer the way I do. Ice fishing and the weather that goes with it are like liver, without which I probably wouldn't appreciate steak. Lacey says this thinking is ridiculous, but Lacey, you must understand, doesn't need to justify the consumption of liver. In fact, she once ordered this bloody, amorphous blob in a restaurant when we were first dating, an act that caused me to quit calling for a couple of months while I reevaluated our relationship.

Saskatchewan's Cree Lake strengthened my "need to be miserable for optimum enjoyment" theory. In late May, Lacey and I flew to this lovely, expansive body of water. Under normal circumstances, our three days at Cree would have been deemed a fun, exciting trip; under the circumstances as they existed, Cree Lake became our absolutely best fly-fishing adventure ever. That's because it started off so badly.

In northern Saskatchewan, ice sometimes remains on the larger lakes until mid-May. That year, it didn't break up until June 1. We arrived June 2. As you can imagine, when you can still see slabs of ice washed up on shore, there is bound to be a nip in the air. This particular nip was so intense, Lacey and I donned every article of clothing we owned before setting out with our guide.

When at last we arrived in the first bay we were to fish, there were already several boats from the same lodge in the vicinity. Our guide, who spoke little English and was somewhat deficient in people skills, said, "Cast here," but my fingers were so numb I could not even pick up my rod. Lacey, who had put a canvas duffel bag over her head to cut the wind in the open boat, could not make her hands work well enough to remove it. After several minutes of muffled conversation, I think she frightened our guide. In any event, he nervously looked around and announced, "We go 'nudder spot."

After going to " 'nudder spot" several times, we still had not thawed out enough to begin fishing. I can't remember being more miserable. When at 11:30 a.m. we stopped for the traditional North Country shore lunch with the other guides and fishermen from the lodge, Lacey and I had no fish to contribute to the meal.

Fortunately, others did. The shore lunch of fresh fried pike fillets, fried potatoes and onions, homemade bread, beans, and green tea is one of the finest traditions of the North Country. On this day, the finest thing about it was the cooking fire. The guides had created an inferno 5 feet wide by 10 feet long that shot flames 8 feet into the air. They carried Lacey and me to within 3 feet and propped us up.

Huge quantities of tea thawed vital internal organs, and in an hour we could feel our fingers. When we took to the water again, we could actually make a few clumsy casts. Nevertheless, the enjoyment was long gone from the day. We considered not going out again.

Luckily, the second and third days were spectacularly dissimilar to the first. Our guide seemed more confident. Twenty-pound pike consistently swirled out of the mud of shallow bays to slam our flies, and a parade of 8- to 12-pound lake trout slammed our gaudy Kokanee smolt patterns.

Lacey insists it became infinitely warmer. Even hot. The fishing, she said, was the best of her life, and I must admit it was glorious. But I still think all that liver on day one had something to do with it.

Relativity

L ife is strange. If you don't believe that, look at my stock holdings. What? You say you can't see my stock holdings? Perhaps that is because they no longer exist. Three years ago at this time I figured that if I didn't take too many exotic fly-fishing trips I could live comfortably until my time ran out. Well, evidently my time has run out. Forget about the new cane 4-weight I've been eyeing. I suppose that if I had to I could be happy with my old graphite rod and a few day trips down to the Big Spokane River. It's all relative anyway.

Relativity is indeed strange. Relativity is feeling so cold you don't think you could feel colder, and then feeling so much colder you wish you could feel cold again. Relativity is experiencing the best time of your life casting flies for 12-pound bonefish in the Florida Keys, then coming home to experience another best time of your life by merely casting a black marabou for small crappie in a city-park pond.

Relativity is what makes a stale doughnut and a lukewarm thermos of coffee taste like prime rib and good Merlot if you are stuck for three hours at dinnertime in Lolo Pass while two wreckers attempt to extract a truck-trailer rig from the Lochsa River. It's what makes a forgotten, lint-covered gummy bear from your fishing vest taste like a Full Meal Deal when you've been fishing six hours on Crab Creek in late December and your lunch is still back home on the kitchen counter.

The first time I went to Alaska, I was afraid I had absolutely destroyed my fishing future in the Lower 48. How could one possibly fight daily battles with powerful, stubborn kings and 15-pound tail-walking silvers, then return to Loon Lake and its 10-inch rainbows? I figured once I got home, I'd never enjoy Loon Lake again.

On several evenings last summer, however, I paddled my belly boat parallel to the railroad tracks at Loon, offering a size-14 Adams to the small rainbows dimpling the water. I had a ball. My whoops were no less loud or enthusiastic than those I emitted on the Kenai River near Soldotna, Alaska, when a 60-pound salmon hammered my fluorescent red marabou and threatened to pull me from my tenuous perch on some rocks above the water. I caught the rainbow on 2-pound tippet and the king salmon on a 20. For the trout I used a little bamboo 4-weight. For the king I had a 10-weight graphite and a multiplier reel. Relativity.

Life is full of such oddities. Have you ever noticed how long it takes to get to the Seep Lakes near Moses Lake if the Seep Lakes are your final destination, and how quickly you pass by if you are driving west from Spokane and your final destination is Puget Sound? How about the fact that hot dogs taste twice as good over a smudgy fire in fishing camp, or that no matter who catches the largest brown, yours put up a better fight?

Most important, perhaps, is that the wives of die-hard fly fishermen evidently prefer our gusto for life over someone else's dashing good looks. This is a tremendous comfort to those among us with beer bellies, plumber's butt, and bird legs. I don't know if that is a statement about a woman's eyesight or her ability to see beyond the cover of the book, but I think it, also, has to do with relativity.

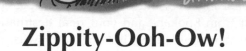

Zippity-Ooh-Ow!

◆

Buttons make a lot of sense, and it looks as if other fastening devices, such as Velcro and those plastic three-pronged snaps, have found a permanent home in the fishing industry. What I want to know, though, is what genius invented the zipper? I'm serious. What kind of mind would say, "If I do this and this and this, people will be able to fasten their pants without using safety pins." Certainly, zippers are too complicated to have been invented by accident, as were penicillin and Silly Putty.

For me, zippers are still about the handiest of all fastening devices. They keep my neoprene jacket closed against the elements, help my waders go on and off easily, and make assorted fanny and backpacks easily and quickly accessible. I keep some of my fly rods in a zippered cloth case. Nevertheless, I have always had a love/hate relationship with zippers. My primary complaint is that when a zipper malfunctions, the thing it is on becomes pretty much useless.

Most salespersons nowadays will tell you it is cheaper to replace a garment than to replace the zipper. That may be so for an

$8 sweatshirt, but I can't believe they want me to throw out my $369 wet suit just because the zipper quit zipping.

Perhaps even more irritating than zippers that quit working are zippers that only work occasionally. These are the ones that function just fine one time, then come undone from the bottom the next time. There are few things that make a guy look dorkier than a nice canvas fishing vest or waterproof jacket that is unzipping from the bottom up.

Fixing such a malfunction is difficult and awkward and time consuming, and removing the garment without unzipping it is even worse. I once took out a whole row of tables at a nice little outdoor café after a day of fishing the Sand River. It had warmed up nicely, and I was trying to remove a light jacket with a stuck zipper. In anger, I finally attempted to pull it off over my head, but I got tangled in it, lost my sight and my balance, and went into a power spin.

I think the waiters at the café thought I was part of the mime group performing on the patio, as they laughed, clapped, and helped me up without so much as an angry word about the sorry condition of their tables. Afterwards, I didn't have sense enough to throw the jacket out—I spent a half hour working the zipper down to the bottom and off. That way, the next time I wanted to wear it, I had forgotten about the malfunction and was able to repeat my frenzied escape attempts in another public place.

The worst experience I ever had with a zipper was one night in Eddie Schlick's backyard when several of us were staying over to sleep under the stars. We had been casting homemade poppers for big bluegills in the pond behind his house, and after roasting wieners for dinner we decided to go skinny-dipping in the same pond. Afterwards, I dove into my sleeping bag and zipped it up, catching a very important part of my budding masculinity in the zipper.

The worse part was I was screaming so loudly no one really knew what the problem was, and before I could attempt to free myself, Eddie called his mom out to the backyard. Mrs. Schlick, bless her heart, freed me with a minimum of commotion and only a few giggles, but I never could look her in the face after that, and I never asked to fish the pond again.

Advice for Seth

❖

Well, I finally got to welcome a son-in-law, Seth, into the family, and I think he's a keeper. Any man who can make my daughter say she will try trout fishing has got to have his ducks in a row. If he can teach her to cook trout, he'll really have accomplished something.

I think Jennifer got turned off on both fishing and eating fish at an early age when I was doing a lot of fly fishing for carp. They were big, golden, mud-gobbling things from the Long Lake sloughs, and I probably should have left them in the water. I didn't, though, bringing the things home and experimenting with different recipes. I'd heard folks in Europe liked carp, a consideration that eventually confirmed my opinion that European culinary preferences are somewhat primitive.

Jennifer would groan and pick at her fish and beg for a hotdog, but I made her try the carp. To encourage her, I'd take a piece myself and pretend it wasn't making me sick. Sometimes it stayed down, but I remember most vividly the times it didn't.

I feel it is my obligation as a new father-in-law to share some insights about my baby girl with her new husband. First off, she is terribly competitive. She was an excellent basketball player in high school and still has a great touch. Seth probably already knows about that. At least I hope so. A great touch can make up for all sorts of deficiencies in the kitchen.

Jennifer will probably be a very good fly fisher. I know a few fellows who still judge both their self-worth and their virility by whether they cast better than the next guy, and I trust Seth is not one of them. He must just try to remember there are other things he and I do well that she will never do—even a few that have nothing to do with muscle mass or plumbing.

My little girl will most likely drive Seth nutty at first with her early-morning routine. She has always been a bit obsessed about makeup and wearing coordinated "outfits." When she was in grade school, she wouldn't leave the house unless her Flintstones sweatshirt blended nicely into her burgundy leotards.

If Seth ever gets her to pull on a pair of hip waders and a yellow raincoat, he'll know she is coming around. If he can then convince her that a hat and mosquito dope preclude the need for all makeup, she won't have to get up at midnight to be ready for a 4 a.m. departure.

Another thing Seth probably needs to know about my daughter is that she doesn't like to be cold. I am partly to blame for this, as I often took her snow sledding when she was a tyke, and she really wasn't very well outfitted. She still puts on a jacket if the temperature dips below 70 degrees. If he ever takes her out in early spring, he will need to invest in multiple hand warmers, several thermoses, and at least one hot water bottle. Being newly married, he'll probably think of some other stuff to keep her warm, too.

I am looking forward to Jen and Seth's first fly-fishing trip over here. If the two of them can come in August, I'll bet we can find some cutthroat on the St. Joe River. If they come later, we might try for steelhead on the Clearwater. I doubt we will fish for carp, though, and if we do, we for sure won't be eating them.

Travelin' Easy

❖

A fishing partner's father has a warm ritual for guests about to leave his home to drive long distances back to theirs. First, he fixes them a toasted fried-egg-and-mayonnaise sandwich, which he wraps in a napkin. Then he walks them to their vehicle, pats the fender softly, and utters these optimistically benevolent words: "Travel easy, my friend."

Don't I wish! For years, the ability to "travel easy" has eluded me. Because of my inherent mechanical deficiencies, I'm in a constant state of angst when I'm on the road in my own vehicle. I don't just fear breaking down on the way to a New Mexico trout stream, I expect it. I sit tensely upright listening to the assorted tinny clashes and growlings that assure me I will eventually be stranded in the middle of the road in the middle of the night in the middle of nowhere. I am absolutely certain car manufacturers have programmed my vehicles so they will self-destruct when I hit the road with a fly rod and a vest on the backseat.

Even if someone else is driving, I find I do not travel all that easy. Ever on the alert, ever valve vigilant, I am also a backseat driver, ever aware of the shortcomings of others.

"Shouldn't you have turned back there?"

"Do you always run this close to the center line?"

The floorboards of my best friend's truck are worn away clear to the metal where I have braked from the passenger's side. In my teenage son's car, where I often need to brake harder, the metal is worn away also, and the asphalt flashes by as he races fate to our next fishing destination.

I admit my inability to "travel easy" is due largely to my inability to ignore insignificant bumps and squeaks and rattles. I admit my paranoias are not only unfounded, they are often ridiculous. Just often enough, though, they are due to circumstances that can't be ignored. Last winter's fly-fishing expedition to Utah's Provo River is an example.

The night before five of us were to leave from Salt Lake City, it snowed 9 inches. What should have been an easy two-hour drive including a stop for breakfast turned into a five-hour creep down a snow-rutted, one-lane freeway while all five of us whined about being hungry and missing the best fishing. Soon, however, we had another problem.

Don, the driver, a fellow I hardly knew, had been duck hunting a few days before, and when he had shed his neoprenes after picking up decoys, he dumped them in the back of his SUV. There, his young Labrador had evidently peed on them during the long drive home. At least that's the way Don figured it later. Now, as they warmed and ripened in the crowded vehicle, they began to emit an eye-watering ammonia smell.

By the time we figured out that the source of the pungent odor was not a bag of salt-and-vinegar potato chips gone bad, my eyes had been rubbed red and I was contemplating walking the rest of the way to Provo alongside the van. In retrospect, this would have been faster and a lot more comfortable.

Don thought the incident funny and was offended when I suggested to him what he could do with both his dog and his neoprenes. There were definitely some hard feelings, and with the passage of time I feel real bad about that. Therefore, I wish to apologize.

Don, I hope you travel as easily as I for the rest of your days.

Phonda Pea

———— ❦ ————

When I was 9, my father talked my Uncle Hank into keeping me on his cattle ranch for a week or so. I had been moody since my girlfriend, Phonda Pea, snuck off with her parents back to Alabama, taking my fly-tying kit with her, and I think my folks just wanted to be alone for a while without having to gaze each morning and evening into my pitiful, petulant face.

When they dropped me off, Mom gave me a hug and told me to stay away from the gravel-pit pond, so, with nothing else to do, I spent the next day perched on a fence post complaining to cows. I found them to be intrinsically compassionate about matters of the heart.

After a few more days of such excitement, the pond began calling to me. "Jimmm-mmy," it would say, "I'm over he-errre. Your mo-therrr will ne-verr knowww." Though my name wasn't Jimmy, you couldn't expect a gravel-pit pond to remember everything. That night, I "went out to talk to the cows" and slipped furtively across the back 40 to the 5-acre impoundment. As I gazed across the moon-slickened water, a large fish rose in the exact center, creating golden, concentric ripples that spread themselves thin before being gobbled up by the cattails. Now here, I remember thinking, is a good thing. I need to cast a fly over this pond.

Somewhere I had read about men who built and named magnificent sailing craft after women who had jilted them. In this manner, they prolonged their delicious misery. As far as I could tell, no one had ever been as miserable as I, having suffered the heartache of losing both a girl and a fly-tying kit in the same night. Certainly I qualified to build something—at least a raft—and so what if it doubled as a fishing boat?

I spent a couple of afternoons buried in the cattails, lashing some of my uncle's just-delivered fence posts together with baling wire.

I didn't think he'd mind too terribly much that I'd borrowed the posts, but I wasn't certain enough about it to ask. In the process of building the raft, which I named *Phonda Pea* (of course!), fishing had become a secondary consideration.

"Well, Uncle Hank," I said after dinner the next night, "I guess I'll wander out and talk with the cows a spell." *Phonda Pea* was ready to be launched.

Uncle Hank dug a toothpick into a back molar and leaned back. "You do that, boy," he said, "but don't be too long. Your daddy called a bit ago and he'll be out shortly to pick you up."

A half hour before dark, my father and my uncle found me. They had already checked the pasture and the chicken house and were taking long, angry strides when I saw them approaching. I had to hurry. I had just finished dragging *Phonda Pea* into the water, so I quickly climbed aboard and pushed off. I would take my punishment, but first I would take a farewell cruise.

Phonda Pea drifted toward the center of the pond, riding well. "She's fine!" I screamed. "She's really fine! I didn't think she would be but she is, and now I'm leavin' but at least I said goodbye and I didn't steal no fly-tying kit neither!"

On the ride home, my father kept casting sideways glances at me as I leaned back next to him on the front seat, sometimes smiling, sometimes wiping away tears. He said he understood, and maybe he did, but I think he suspected sunstroke. In any event, he promised to buy me another fly-tying kit, and he never did tell my mother.

All Planes Land

O ne night a year ago, I was grappling with some periodic blahs and evaluating the quality of the life I had lived. While I was dwelling on the fact that my "three score and seven" was significantly closer than the day of my birth, my alter ego perched on my pillow.

"Miserable, ain'tcha?" he said. Alter egos are supposed to be inseparable friends, but mine is a jerk. Has bad grammar, too.

"Go away," I suggested. "I'm trying to sort out my life."

"How're ya doin'?" he persisted. "With sortin' out your life, I mean."

"I've got some regrets," I admitted. "Too many things I haven't done."

"Such as?"

"Such as I've never caught a big pike on a fly," I said. "I've always wanted to take a big northern on a fly. How can I be happy with that on my mind?"

"So why don't you just do it?" my alter ego suggested. "Go to Saskatchewan or Manitoba and take a 25-pounder on a fly."

I jerked my head up. "Do you really think I could?" I asked. "Just like that?"

"Of course," he said. "You can do anything you want. Not well, perhaps, as you have so frequently demonstrated, but I should think you'd be used to that by now."

For a moment I glared at him, wondering if I should be offended. "OK," I growled defiantly. "I'll make reservations tomorrow."

"That's the spirit!" A. E. said. "Drive up there, charter one of those itsy-bitsy bush planes, and fly out to some remote lake."

"Itsy-bitsy planes?" I squeaked. "Fly? On second thought, I've been thinking about buying an exercise bike and..."

"Monster pike," he said, taunting me. "You're not afraid of

airplanes, are you?"

"Only when they're flying," I said.

"Thirty-pounders," he expounded, taunting me some more. "Tackle busters. Regular 'gators."

A month later I was in the air somewhere above northern Saskatchewan, heading for a landing strip on Cree Lake. On one hand, I was elated I had taken the challenge. On the other, I knew I was going to die.

"You can open your eyes now," the pilot said. "We're up."

"I figured that," I said. "Let me know when we're not."

"You'll get used to it pretty soon," the pilot said. "Why don't you open your eyes? It's not good to grit your teeth like that."

With thumb and forefinger I pried one eye partially open and tried to get used to it. I was silent several moments, watching blue water and gray-green tundra slide beneath us. Then I closed my eyes again.

After what seemed a day or two, the pilot nudged me. "Open up," he said. "There it is." He was pointing to a narrow ribbon of gravel carved at the end of an island.

"Well, I'm glad that's over," I sighed. I glanced at the pilot. "Now, one more question." A sense of relief was making me giddy. I knew that if I could get a laugh out of my pilot, life as I had once known it would again be possible. "Can you land this thing?"

The pilot looked back at me solemnly. "All planes eventually land," he said.

I gulped and became quiet again. Maybe I would catch a big pike on a fly and maybe I wouldn't. But I knew for certain I was looking forward to meeting my alter ego again in the safety of my own bedroom. Some things change; some do not. I'd teach the little nuisance not to meddle in my phobias.

Alarming Business

———∽∽∽———

It's 2 a.m. and I can't sleep. The alarm clock was set to go off at 3, but alarm clocks and I have this understanding: I don't have to shut them off and they don't have to work.

It used to be that alarm clocks and I were not nearly so agreeable. It used to be that I regularly chucked ringing alarm clocks across the room and went back to sleep. That was back in my college days, however, when I had a 7 a.m. "Brit Lit" (British literature) class.

With important things like fishing and hunting now more prominent on my daily agenda, I never throw my clock. The mere act of setting the clock, in fact, guarantees I will not need it. If I set an alarm clock, it can only mean that I am getting up early to meet a friend, and I will lie awake all night worrying that the alarm will not sound or that I will not hear it. Oh, how I sometimes wish I were like my brother-in-law, Thayer the Abnormal, who views deadlines the same way he views the Ten Commandments—as suggestions. If Thayer is ready within an hour of the appointed time, he considers it "close enough." I've tried to break him of this habit by leaving him behind when he's not ready. So far he has learned nothing—he just goes happily back to bed.

The possibility of not hearing the alarm has become more likely for me every year. It used to be that a mouse nibbling through a package of spaghetti noodles in the downstairs cupboard at night would cause me to sit bolt upright in bed. Now I think a beaver chomping on the leg of my poster bed would not do the job. Being on time, though, was something my father taught me, so I do what I must to keep from being late—I set the alarm so I will be assured of never falling asleep.

This morning, I shut my alarm clock off two hours before it was set to ring. I am driving several hundred miles with Mike to fish the Saco River in New Hampshire, and he will be here at 4 a.m. This gives me more than an hour to stare at the ceiling before I get up, dress, and cook some breakfast. I hate breakfast at 3 a.m.; I can't eat on an empty stomach, but if I don't eat I'll be burned out before noon. Dad always used to give me oatmeal and toast before we went fishing, but there was no enjoyment in eating. Oatmeal may, in fact, be the reason I do not like breakfast today. "It sticks to your ribs," Dad always used to say. Where it really stuck, though, was in my throat. Then it balled up in my stomach.

By the time Mike gets here, I will finally be sleepy. We will make the drive north on State Route 16, and I will either be slouched down on the seat, snoring, or resting my head against a window, snoring. Mike says he doesn't mind my snoring, except when I'm driving. That's why we usually take his rig. He jokes that although I will someday go peacefully in my sleep, my passengers will not find the end nearly so soothing.

Finally, we will be at the Saco, and I will forget about alarm clocks and oatmeal and Brit Lit and such and begin concentrating on patterns and drifts. My nap will have left me refreshed, and as I cast I'll guiltily consider offering to do the driving on the way home. Then I will notice that Mike is again catching the most fish. Nah—he can drive. He's tougher than I. Why mess with a good thing?

Liquid Sunshine

◆

When I was a child of 3, my father decided it was time I learned to swim. Without consulting Dr. Spock, attending classes in parent-child interdependence, worrying about my psychological adjustment, or attempting to develop rapport with the runny-nosed rug rat he had sired, Dad took me to the end of the Loon Lake dock and dropped me in. Parenting was a lot easier back then.

Though I questioned his intentions at the time, I did learn to tread water, and eventually I earned my lifesaving certification from the YMCA. As was normal in those days, my efforts were directed toward water with horizontal surfaces, such as that in rivers and ponds. Until I fished Washington's Olympic rain forest, in fact, I had never even considered swimming through water that moved vertically.

I was on the Queets River in early March, sliding a small black marabou down the lane at the head of a pool. Talk about rain! With a little latitude from Sir Isaac Newton, I could have dog-paddled through the air back to camp. This was supposed to be a relaxing trip, the culmination of two months of tenacious research and a reward for finishing a book project on time. So far, however, it had been anything but fun.

The night before, I had pitched my dome tent in a nearby campground. Luckily, I was the only one there. I am certain there are activities necessitating more cursing than pitching a tent in a downpour, but I have not tried them yet. And while it is true the procedure might have gone more smoothly had I not left a set of fiberglass "ribs" in the garage back home, it was the constant rain that created the tension. A river only slightly smaller than the Queets itself flowed between my tennis shoes, and, as I attempted to avoid it, I spread my legs farther and farther apart until I looked like the Colossus of Rhodes in a slicker.

An hour later, my tent jury-rigged into a laughable, limp suggestion of habitability, I lay in a half-inch of water and attempted to entice the sandman. I was imagining the headlines in the Seattle papers: FISHERMAN DROWNS IN TENT. Outside, the rain continued its assault. No matter where I moved, I was under a drip.

Drifting at last into soggy slumber, I dreamed fitfully about a Boston Blackie film I had seen as a kid. Blackie had been tied up by a gang of ruthless jewel smugglers who were attempting to relieve him of his stashed diamonds.

"Ve haf vays of making you talk," sneered the ruthless Mr. X.

"Give 'er yer best shot, Bozo," Blackie said defiantly, straining at the ropes. "You ain't gettin' nothin' from me."

Mr. X rubbed his palms together in delight. "Zen you leaf me no choice," he said ominously. "Ze Chinese vater torture!"

Plop. Plop. Plop. Hour after hour, single drops of cold water dripped onto the forehead of my hero until finally . . . "I'll tell, I'll tell!" I screamed, waking myself up. In resignation, I crawled out of the tent, donned a yellow poncho, and spent the rest of the night in soggy, lonely misery, squatting beneath a towering cedar while the rain made puddles all around me.

The 4x4 Fishing Conveyance

❖

George Burns had his cigar. Michael Jordan had his jump shot. I have my truck, "Old Blue." Old Blue defines me; it's who I am.

"You're a hunk of rusted metal that leaks noxious gases?" Lacey sat on the porch swing. She had been thumbing through a copy of *Northwest Fly Fishing* as I tinkered with the truck's taillights. I had just shared what was perhaps the most profound insight of the summer, and she had barely looked up.

"There are 14 years of my life tied up in this old truck," I continued. "We've fished Alaska together three times. We've chased summer chinook and winter steelhead. We've been to weddings and birthings and funerals."

Lacey put the magazine down. "You've been broken down on every back road in the state of Washington," she said. "You've put the children of two mechanics through med school." She wrinkled her nose. "And you never did find that crappie, did you?"

"Lacey," I said hotly, "I guarantee the crappie is not here. While it's true we did keep six crappie and returned with but five that day, it is not still in the truck. Heck, that was more than eight months ago."

"Then what is it I'm always smelling?" she asked. Without waiting for an answer, she went back to her reading.

What, indeed? I thought. What would one expect to smell in a truck used primarily to get from one fishing hole to another? Cappuccino? Orange truffles? Why, an archaeologist could track a quarter of my adult life by excavating under the seat.

Here is my canteen. It doesn't have any water in it because it froze and burst last winter when I was casting nymphs for brown trout on Crab Creek. Sometime this spring, all the water leaked out. Only it wasn't water; it was hot chocolate.

And lookie here. Puffballs. Of course, they don't look like mushrooms now, what with the coating of crushed Cheetos and all, but they were prime when I picked them up by Deer Creek, the same day the brookies were taking dry flies behind the beaver dam. I completely forgot about the mushrooms once they rolled off the seat.

Now, here's something I've been missing for a long time: the marshmallow Easter bunny Rachel gave me. Spring of '98, as I recall. Right before the drive up to Pettit Lake. Looks kind of bad, doesn't it? The dog will love it.

A bologna sandwich? Or is it peanut butter? I'd probably better not give this one to the dog. Hey, here's Mike's missing fly box. Don't know what this is wrapped around it, though. Could be my handkerchief. Might be a banana peel. Smells like cod liver oil.

See the tooth marks here? Sis did that when she was just a pup. She lay there on the passenger's side floor and I thought she was being so good, and the whole time she was chewing on the oil container. That's why it's empty. I can imagine where the oil ended up. That's probably another reason these mushrooms look so bad.

A working vehicle is *supposed* to have a distinctive aroma. And that's just part of what I love about this truck. Oh sure, most folks look at it and see a 14-year-old wreck with a missing fuse panel cover and a missing gearshift knob. I look at it as a 4x4 fishing conveyance rife with memories. And it just so happens that the fuse panel and gearshift knob are right here under the seat.

Hmmmm. What the heck! Well, I'll be jiggered. "Lacey! I found that crappie!"

Hot Tubbing

Owning a hot tub was never one of my life goals. Heck, as a kid I quit taking Saturday-night baths because, as I eloquently explained to my mother, "I ain't sittin' in that used water no more." Now, in the name of hot tubbing, I hope to sit in used water several times a week. The amount of soaking time, you see, is in direct proportion to the number of times I go winter fishing.

When Lacey and I bought a hot tub, we thought it would be romantic on a cold December night after a successful foray out to Crab Creek—snow floating down from an ebony sky and all that. It is romantic, too—until Lacey gets claustrophobic from the heat and runs into the house, playfully suggesting I follow. Before doing so, I must put the bubble cover and lid back on. Let me tell you, the romance goes away very quickly when you are sopping wet, the wind chill is below zero, and you are fighting with a bubble cover that won't lie flat. When you have completed the onerous task and then have to run all the way around the house to the front because your wife has inadvertently locked the back door, all amorous thoughts are replaced with open hostility.

Romance aside, the hot tub was still a good idea for therapeutic reasons after a winter fly-fishing expedition. As I grow older, my body has quit responding favorably to walking long distances in neoprene. This is contrary to the "stay active—stay young" philosophy imparted by doctors in their 30s who have never laid in bed in the morning after a day of wading a cold, rocky river and wondered how they were going to get to the bathroom under their own power.

Some people say a hot tub is difficult to maintain, but ours has stayed pretty clean, except for the time last spring I was practicing casting a weighted size-2 Polar Shrimp in the backyard and the backcast of my aborted double haul landed in the tub where my sister-in-law was soaking. That in itself didn't cause any problems; the problem arose when the angry forward cast snagged her halter top, ripped it loose, and sailed it into the middle of the lawn. When Margaret started screaming, Sis the Lab came to attention from where she had been lying on the patio. When I retrieved the yellow halter and tossed it with gallant apologies back into the tub, the dog thought it was her tennis ball and dove in after it. Sis had been digging gophers in the garden an hour earlier, and when she hit the water, it immediately took on the color of hot chocolate. We ended up having to drain the tub.

Other than that, we enjoy our hot tub after a day of winter fly fishing. Any negativism I might project here is merely a matter of getting off on the wrong foot. Before the tub could be installed, Lacey and I had to build a patio to put it on, arranging a dozen heavy railroad ties as a border, sledge-hammering away a cement slab, hauling out a truckload of sod, wheelbarrowing in two yards of sand, and then laying 438 pavers, leveling each one individually. We spent a lot of time on our knees and a lot of time with a shovel. We didn't fish for two weeks, and at the end of each day we were so sore we could barely eat. I guess I've always resented the fact that the hot tub wasn't there when we needed it most.

The Tub

❖

M y first fishing boat was an 8-foot wooden pram, nearly as wide as it was long. My Uncle Pat called it a "widow maker," but come April it carried Jerry and Eddie and me frequently and safely (but perhaps not so wisely) through a stretch of fast water on the Big Spokane River to a deep hole next to a gravel shelf on the east bank. There, beneath the overhanging willows, rainbow trout found the living easy.

None of us had a truck in those days, so the boat we took to calling "The Tub" was secured to the top of my 1961 Volkswagen Beetle with a couple hundred feet of cotton rope. When we arrived at our pull-off beside the river, looking like a rolling spider web, we were always obliged to spend the next 20 minutes liberating "The Tub" from her confines—not an easy task with six thumbs working feverishly in the dark against the inevitability of dawn's first hatch. When at last she was free, we loaded her with fly rods and lunches, and slid her down the bank to the dark water.

When I look back on those days, I am most gratefully reminded that God does indeed watch over children, dumb animals, and fools. We were not small boys. Jerry, in fact, was pushing 280 pounds, and Eddie and I were both over 200. With less than an inch of freeboard between us and the swirling river, we motored through the early-morning mist to our secret honey hole.

The trout were big (more than 8 inches) and sassy, and they rose with abandon to nearly every fly we threw. The limit was 12 a day back then, which times three came to 36 fish. And that was always our goal. We were young and stupid and truly believed we could do this for the rest of our lives. Deplete the resource? What's a resource, mister?

In her third spring, we left "The Tub" chained to a tree beside the river one afternoon because we intended to fish the next day too. The following morning, as usual, we launched in the near dark, but only a few yards from shore we were in water to our ankles. Sabotaged! Someone had knocked a softball-size hole in the bottom of my pram, right beneath a seat. The three of us made it back with most of our gear, but my beautiful wooden vessel disappeared silently and forlornly beneath the water.

Today, I own a collapsible 12-foot Porta-Bote, which I strap to the top of my truck when I head north to the pike and grayling waters of the Yukon. I keep a 16-foot fiberglass Coleman canoe behind the shed for summer fly-fishing floats down the Little Spokane and the Winchester Wasteway. In the carport sits my close-to-home and saltwater boat, a 16-foot Lund Renegade with an 80-horse Yamaha. Next to that is my duck boat, an 18-foot camouflaged Lowe with an 18-horse Mercury outfitted to carry me comfortably into the sand dunes of Potholes Reservoir. I love them all.

Yes, a lot has changed since my three years with "The Tub." The gravel shelf is still there across the river, but the willows fell victim several years ago to an overzealous beaver, and the old launching spot is now part of someone's front yard.

I hardly ever see a native rainbow anymore. Many days, as I trailer my Lund downstream toward the fancy cement launch, I think about progress and my evolution as a boat owner and fisherman, and I wonder if I didn't love "The Tub" best of all.

The Exaggerators

❖

Once a week, for about a year now, three fishing friends and I have met for lunch. We were pretty thick back in the mid–'60s, frequenting local waters and watering holes. There was a lot of good-natured competition then, and a fair number of preposterous stories, and it has been good to be together again so many years later, having at last become what we were to become.

I don't think my friends and I consciously try to fool one another now, but I do think that if you tell the same lies over and over again, you begin to believe them yourself. I, for example, have always had a tendency to exaggerate the accuracy of my fly casting. I am not an absolutely terrible caster, but I have noticed that, just when I think I'm finally in a groove, I will suddenly start impaling body parts and trees. During our lunches, if a little creative forgetfulness on my end puffs me up a bit, I'll become creatively forgetful.

Paul also tells lies—but they are mostly to himself. Paul used to be the best fly fisherman of us all, but he now has numerous medical problems exacerbated by alcohol abuse. He is prone to self-diagnosis that never suggests exercise, a better diet, and less bending of the elbow would bring him back to his previous proficiency and make him love the sport again.

Another friend, Ronald, weaves elaborate tales and is, out of habit, a master of one-upmanship. If you own a nice split-bamboo rod, Ronald owns the factory. If your drift boat cost two grand, Ronald's is priceless. Ronald spins yarns that tread on the toes of credulity, but he never crosses the fine line between what is almost believable and what is ludicrous. Is it possible that under a pen name he actually does write magazine articles about exotic fly-fishing destinations? Is it possible he is really part owner of a particularly fine fly-fishing lodge in the Bahamas, or that he fishes with Bill Gates, or that he has a ranch in Colorado and a condo in Maui? Of course it isn't, but I don't question him, and sometimes I find myself making up preposterous tales of my own just so I can listen to Ronald gleefully do me one better.

Kent, my third luncheon friend, makes no effort to make his stories believable. Never has. I used to resent that somewhat, as I thought it implied he thought me either extremely gullible or exceedingly stupid. Perhaps he does, but now I eagerly await the airing of his fantasies. Kent's tales are so preposterous it is difficult not to laugh before he finishes. At our last get-together, he (with a straight face) told us of sitting down on a rock while changing flies on the Beaver Kill and having the "rock" turn into a very large, very angry black bear.

Kent has also been chased by snakes that have taken their tails in their mouths and rolled after him down a hill. He found a quarter-pound gold nugget while fishing the Kenai River, and kept it several years "for luck" in his fly vest. Sadly, he lost it in an avalanche in Louisiana. There was no explanation as to why he kept the nugget in his fly vest, or how he managed to get caught in an avalanche in a state where the highest "mountain" is man-made.

As with the others, I don't know why I like Kent, but I do. I guess that's the way it is with friends.

The Movie Maker

I was recently forced to endure one of my more miserable social experiences of the year: a narrated, three-hour home video of a San Juan River fishing trip.

Normally, a video of a premier New Mexico fly-fishing river would have me sitting on the edge of my seat in anticipation. For a man who loves both the quarry and the process and has been briefly tantalized by the beauty of the San Juan, this should have been at least interesting. It wasn't. For three interminable hours, I shredded paper napkins, cleaned my fingernails with a fork, and counted things. I counted chairs, tables, and tiles on the ceiling. I counted ice cubes in the water pitcher and the number of times the narrator said, "Um," and scratched himself below the belt.

The video in question had multiple problems, not the least of which was the fact I was stuck in the middle of a crowded banquet room with no graceful means of escape. Other problems were technical in nature, such as the fact that the cameraman "friend" of the fisherman appeared to have done his filming in poor light while jumping on a trampoline, and the fact that the time and date were flashing in the lower left corner of the film. At one point this reminded me that though this was a five-day trip, we were only up to the blurs comprising day two.

"See that?" the narrator enthused while showing one particularly violent session on the trampoline. "That's a 9-pound brown. Took him on a size-16 Gray Caddis."

As a matter of fact, I didn't see "that." What I saw was a dark, blocky apparition with no distinguishing features stuck in what might have been a landing net. Or perhaps it was on a barbecue. The apparition could have been a football, a large venison roast, or even a Ping-Pong paddle.

"How about that New Mexico moon?" the narrator said a

little while later.

Imagine that, I thought, looking up from my shredded napkins. It looks just like a Colorado moon, only blurrier.

The video went on and on, one shaky image after another. My head was pounding from trying to focus, and my other senses were complaining too. Not only was this fellow's friend a poor videographer, but he didn't know a thing about fishing. I could just see him running along the stream in flip-flops with a camcorder in one hand and a glass of wine in the other.

The final lowlight of the video came when the narrator and his buddy came across a deep pool into which was inserted the very tip of the camcorder lens wrapped in cellophane. For 10 minutes, the audience was assured there were "big fish down there," but the video might just as well have been shot in a hot tub. I mean, bubbles are bubbles.

Finally, just as I was contemplating slithering across the floor to unplug the television, the video abruptly ended. There was a smattering of applause. I glanced around at my fellow sufferers. Those who weren't asleep looked about sheepishly. "Did we really sit through that?" they seemed to be asking.

On the drive home, I wondered how I should have handled the situation. It struck me that my silence suggested approval, even though I was both offended and bored. With no negative input, the poor narrator will probably show his video again. Next time, however, his audience may rise up and stone him. Do I want that on my conscience? You bet I do!

Over the Bar

❖

In a short time, the coho salmon will again be gathering in the dark, turbulent salt near Buoy 10 at the mouth of the Columbia River. They will stay there, just inside the infamous ship grave-yard known as "The Bar," feeding and socializing and perhaps even contemplating the intelligence of eventually swimming up the Columbia and its tributaries to spawn—a fishy act that amounts to beating yourself up for several weeks just to have a few hours of rather nonintimate sex before dying.

With its tunnel vision, a sexually mature salmon is not all that different from a sexually mature teenager, but for the salmon, sex is a self-destructive process. It is for a teenager, too—but it some-times takes longer. Tragically for the fish, there are no elders, no matriarchs or patriarchs to guide them or to even answer questions about the perilous journey; these are the matriarchs and patriarchs, for salmon do not survive their initial sexual experience. That's why you never hear a big buck coho bragging about his prowess with the hens.

Suppose, however, that one salmon did survive the spawning ritual to return to the ocean. Imagine the conversation this mentor salmon would have with the younger fish:

Mentor salmon: "Johnny, if you go ahead and follow your friends up that river, you will encounter uncountable dangers. There will be fishermen with rods and nets and all sorts of badly tied imitations. There will be wild otters and bears, eagles and rac-coons. You will be required to swim up rapids, jump up waterfalls, swim miles and miles and miles—all without any snacking."

Johnny: "No snacking! Whoa! No herring? No squid?"

Mentor salmon: "That's right, Johnny. And when you finally get to where you are going, your beautiful skin will have turned a dull red, your teeth will protrude grotesquely, and there will be ugly wounds and patches of fungus all over your body."

Johnny: "Zits! No way! Chicks don't dig zits, and I just got my braces off. To heck with this—I'm heading back to the Bering Sea."

Mentor salmon (encouraged): "That's a good boy, Johnny. Spawning just isn't worth it."

Johnny: "Spawning? Isn't that like sex? There's going to be sex?"

Mentor salmon: "Terrible rapids and raging waterfalls, Johnny."

Johnny: "Sex?"

Mentor salmon: "No herring, Johnny. Yucky fungus and lots of owies."

Johnny: "Sex with girls?"

Mentor salmon (with growing resignation): "Girl salmon, Johnny. Nasty, fishy-smelling things with big teeth and distended bellies. A one-night stand at best. Then, you die. It's not all it's cracked up to be."

Johnny: "Sex with girl salmon! I'm heading out tonight."

Mentor salmon (sighing): "I figured as much, Johnny." He turns and swims slowly away, then turns. "Johnny . . ."

"What?"

"Be a good boy."

Johnny grins and pumps a fin. "Hey, Ralphie," he calls to a friend swimming by. "It's a road trip, man!"

The mentor salmon sighs again and heads back into the Pacific toward Buoy 17. He is filled with self-doubt. Was it really so bad, this spawning thing? He is thinking maybe he should give it one more chance.

Arizona Time

❧

I am fairly certain I am the only remaining inhabitant of this planet who still thinks 9:30 means 9:30 rather than sometime between 9:35 and 11:00. I'm beginning to wonder if this is a serious character defect—always being on time.

When I was in college, my roommate, Jim, and I used to double-date a couple of gals who liked fly fishing almost as much as we did. But while I was out warming up the car, Jim was still inside dressing either his line or himself. This disturbed me terribly as good dates of any sort were hard for me to find, and I especially didn't want to jeopardize my opportunities with members of the female fly-fishing fraternity by missing the evening hatch.

It finally occurred to me that the only way Jim and I would ever pick up our dates on time was for me to tell him we had to be there a half hour earlier than what I'd told the girls. This pretty much put us at their front door right on time, which meant we only had to wait for them an additional 20 minutes. See how it works?

Jim eventually moved to Arizona, and his passion is casting streamers for striped bass on Lake Havasu. On a recent business trip to his town, I stayed with Jim and his wife, Marge, and Jim suggested that he and I do some fishing. Of course, that was something I had anticipated doing in Arizona anyway, but not with Jim. When he invited me to fish with him, in fact, my blood pressure immediately went through the roof. This is because punctuality still means nothing to my friend. I accuse him of being on something I call "Arizona Time," which runs much later than Liere time.

On Liere Time, you set your alarm for 5:00 a.m. so you can leave the house by 5:30 a.m. so you can easily make the 40-mile drive to the charter boat and be there in time for your 6:30 a.m. reservations. The extra few minutes allow for adverse traffic and weather conditions.

On Jim's Arizona Time, you also set the alarm for 5:00 a.m. and get up, but after that all similarities cease to exist.

At 5:15, Jim wandered into the kitchen to make a pot of coffee. I was sitting by the door, ready to go.

At 5:25, he started surfing through the weather channels. I went out and loaded my gear into the car.

At 5:45, Jim asked me if I wanted breakfast. I gave an obscene reply and plopped myself down on the couch. Jim told me to relax.

At 5:50, Jim poured himself a bowl of cereal and opened his e-mail. I contemplated strangling him with the computer cord.

At 6:00, Jim announced we were ready to go. Then he spent 10 minutes looking for his rod while I waited for him in the car.

At 6:55, we arrived at the dock on Lake Havasu—almost a half hour late. The charter captain was nowhere in sight.

"See there!" I complained. "We're late again. The guy went home. We drove all this way for nothing!"

Jim poured a cup of coffee from his thermos and sat down on a bucket. "Relax," he said again.

At 7:15, the charter captain walked down the dock with a handful of fishing rods. "You guys are early," he said.

"You said 6:30," I told him irritably.

"Right," he said, looking at his watch. "You're early."

From his bucket, Jim smiled knowingly and sipped his coffee. He has learned something I will never accept: everyone but me is on Arizona Time.

Absentminded Me

—᠅—

I have been sitting at this computer, staring at a blank screen for 20 minutes now, and it has suddenly occurred to me that I don't know why. Did I come here to write an article for *Eastern Fly Fishing*, was I going to check my e-mail, or did I automatically stop here on my way to the bathroom?

That, of course, raises another disturbing possibility—if I was on my way to the bathroom, why do I now feel no "calling"? I had an uncle who thought the whole world was his bathroom. He was 102, and I can tell you, the city librarian really hated to see him walk in the door.

To make matters even more confusing, I have a whole peanut-butter-and-grape-jelly sandwich in one hand and one that is partially eaten in the other. The one I am eating is thinner than the other and . . . well, what do you know—I put the two jelly sides together!

My friends say I am not losing my mind—they too find themselves in rooms with no apparent motivation for being there. I wonder, though, if they also find themselves eating jelly-and-jelly sandwiches. I wonder if they ever find themselves in the basement with a fly reel in one hand and a box of Orville Redenbacher popcorn in the other? I wonder if they invite people for a fresh fish fry and then go to a movie on the designated evening?

It is embarrassing to have to preface every story with "I probably already told you this, but . . ." I have a lot of good fishing stories I'm sure not everyone has heard, but I can't remember who I told them to.

My doctor, a fly fisherman, says that mental exercise—such as recalling rivers and reciting the type of hackle in my 20 favorite dry flies—will slow down the progression of dementia. Still, I am anxious about it. My mother, bless her heart, could hide her own

Easter eggs, but right up to the end she could recite the name of every lake we ever fished.

Never a very organized person, I have found that I must now write everything down. When I'm leaving town for a few days on an extended fishing trip, I make grocery lists, I make clothing lists, I make tackle lists. My desk calendar is full of detailed notes regarding appointments and times. Were it not for this, I would show up on Mossy Creek when I was supposed to meet friends on Oil Creek, several states away.

When you are absentminded, you need to surround yourself with people who are not. Having absentminded friends is not good. Neither are absentminded doctors or dentists. If my dentist tried to fit me with false teeth and I was in the office to pick up some floss for tying my special bluegill bug, he would lose a lot of credence.

I do not want to entrust my health to a doctor who doesn't remember my name, or loan my favorite 3-weight to a friend who forgets where he got it. On the other hand, it would not be wise to loan me your copy of *A Good Life Wasted* or bring a birthday cake to my house in your favorite pan. You may get them back, but more than likely you'll need to attend my garage sale to do so. I think I'm having one next week . . . or did I already say that?

Oh Lord, I Have Fallen

◆

I am 6 feet, 4 inches tall—half inseam and half muscle spasm. The old-world genes that blessed me with long legs also cursed me with a bad back. Indeed, bad backs have been a Liere family attribute for three generations, as constant as our punctuality and our bald heads.

It is nearly impossible to adequately describe lower back spasms to someone who has never experienced one. Over the years, my proclivity for seizing up has caused me no small amount of discomfort and embarrassment. It has also ruined a number of fly-fishing trips. There is something about the rocking motion in casting a 5-weight that eventually makes my lower back feel like someone is giving me a massage with ice tongs. It doesn't happen all the time, but it happens often enough to make booking an extended trip a gamble. With a really intense lower back spasm, it is impossible to remain upright or to even communicate except in groans and gasps, most of which begin with the same sound a quarterback makes as he coughs up the football after being blindsided by a 240-pound linebacker.

Not all of my lower back pains are so debilitating, but many mornings I have worked up a sweat just sitting on the edge of the bed trying to lasso my toe with the leg hole of my briefs. In the middle of the steelhead season this year, my lower back spasms were so intense I eventually abandoned all hope of dressing myself, bundled up my clothes, and drove to my friend Mike's house, wearing only the T-shirt I already had on. When he finished laughing, he helped me dress. Personally, I didn't find any humor in the situation at all; it was darn cold driving through town like that, and I was worried about what I'd say if I was stopped by the sheriff.

As inconvenient as that would have been, it couldn't have held a candle to the embarrassment generated by the muscle spasm that grabbed me in church last autumn, a week after spending four days with friends on the South Platte. The Reverend Bertram Sinn had just completed his sermon and had called for testimonials from the congregation. While several parishioners stood to share their stories, I bent down to search for the pledge card I had dropped. With my head practically between my legs, my muscles contracted with a jolt of electricity. I gave a loud grunt, followed by an oath as I flopped out of my pew into the aisle.

Through a fog of pain, I could hear people gasping. "What's that guy doin'?" the little girl behind me loudly asked her mother.

"I think he's got the spirit, honey," the mother said in awe.

"Uunnngghh!" I said. My eyes squinted and my teeth clenched, and I tried to roll over.

Reverend Sinn, I was told later, practically raced down the aisle, his face beaming. He firmly grasped my shoulders, and I think he was about to say something religious and profound when I uttered something human and unchurchly.

"Did the spirit want him to say that, Mommy?" the little girl asked. Reverend Sinn had fallen back in surprise and stood at mid-aisle, shaking his head. Then he began to chuckle. "Been fly fishing again?" he asked sympathetically.

"Uunnngghh," I replied.

"The same thing happens to me if I use anything bigger than a 5-weight," he said. Then he rose. "Let us sing," he called. "We'll dedicate this one to Brother Liere—page 148—'O Lord, I Have Fallen Again.' "

The Whole of It

❖❖❖

A minute after the needle goes in and the doctor goes out, my right thumb still throbs terribly. I am sitting on the crisp white paper of the examination table in Room 6B, wondering why there is always crisp white paper on examination tables. I suspect it is to monitor my movement here within the emergency ward, to make sure I don't make good my threat to flee. As long as I sit still, thumb up and legs swinging down, as long as the paper doesn't rustle, the hidden microphones will assure Dr. Big Brother that I have not escaped to the Big Pool on Tekoe Creek while he drinks coffee and jokes with the nurses.

I should be out there, you know, sucking in the stuffed-turkey aroma of damp sage while I prepare to combat the monster brown trout I had seen the day before, hiding just behind the old beaver lodge. Those fish will be sucking down crawdads in another hour, and I've got a big deer-hair fly they won't be able to resist. I've come too far to miss this. How long have I been here now? One hour? Two?

As if I don't have worries enough, here is another: how will I explain this gaping thumb wound to my fishing buddies back home across the mountains? Mauled by a cat, I will say. Perhaps they will assume it was large—a bobcat at the very least—not the ungrateful, 8-pound leashed kitty I had attempted to liberate from a tug-of-war between a stray Lab and my cousin's golden retriever. They will not be sympathetic to a kitty-cat bite. They will make horrible jokes.

A nurse finally appears. She asks if the thumb is numb yet and I say yes, though it will never be numb enough for what she has in mind—Betadine and a scrub brush. I look the other way and grimace while she does her job. The trout will be cruising in another 50 minutes. She is chatting happily about the last patient with a cat bite on his thumb. The infection was horrible, she says. It fused the knuckle. Nice to know.

My daughter-in-law is sitting next to me, talking calmly. She is asking again why it is so important that I be there. Because, I tell her—this is what I do. Do you think I drove all this way merely to see my grandchildren? It is unthinkable that I might miss the first day of a short, three-day trip.

The doctor wanders in and examines me roughly. No stitches, he says; the risk of infection is too great. He lets me go with a white blimp of gauze encasing my right thumb. "Keep it clean, dry, and elevated," he warns. I promise him I will. I'd promise him anything.

A half hour later, I am a quarter mile off Road 2. My first cast brings forth a tiny speck of red, which slowly spreads out to saturate the tip of my white blimp. It is difficult to keep it elevated and strip line at the same time. And it's getting wet. I muff the second cast and put my crawdad imitation in a Russian olive. It takes two minutes to free, and the blimp on my finger is throbbing.

No matter. The browns are still cruising the shadows and the sage is still pungent. A jarring hit and a slugfest put a 20-something-incher in my net. After a time, the thumb is but a small snag in the stream of my consciousness as the evening flows happily onward.

Ol' Gabe

I have never used the services of a fly-fishing guide for trout. Partly, this is because I take pride in my own ability to find fish, match the hatch, and make the presentation. Largely, however, it is because I don't have even the most common vessel in which to urinate, and fishing guides are not nearly as important to my family as toothpaste and stove oil.

Once, when I had decided that catching a really big brown trout from the Colville River on a fly was all that stood between me and eternal fulfillment, a friend tried to help.

"I've got a buddy, Ol' Gabe, from up near Colville, who said he'd show you some monster browns," he said. "He's a part-time guide. No charge for you, though."

I met Ol' Gabe the next morning, and though he was younger than I and was wearing flip-flops, he was on time and seemed to be a nice enough fellow.

After getting lost twice in the space of a half hour, Ol' Gabe finally found the river and started upstream. Before we had walked a quarter mile, he stopped abruptly. "See that?" he whispered, pointing to a shallow pool behind what had once been a beaver dam.

"See what?" I whispered back.

"That brown," he said. "By the white rock. A 5-pounder."

I adjusted my polarized glasses. "That pool isn't 2 inches deep," I said, "and I don't see anything but sticks. Should I cast?"

Gabe's eyes narrowed; he smirked, and shook his head. "I thought you wanted a big one," he said.

"Five pounds is big enough," I admitted.

Gabe didn't seem to hear. He snorted, turned, and continued up the river.

Twice more in the next half hour, my guide insisted he saw fish—another 5-pounder, and one much larger. "Can't you see it?" he asked.

"Just sticks and rock," I said. I made a few casts anyway into some unlikely-looking water while my guide flip-flopped along.

Soon, Gabe's "trout" began to rise. I'd be creeping along behind him, trying to make out fishy shadows, when he'd stop and drop to a knee. "Up there," he'd say.

"Where?"

"Up there by the big stump. A 10-pounder just took a mayfly."

I'd strain my eyes. Not even a breeze disturbed the surface. No mayflies either. "I don't see anything," I'd say.

Gabe would look at me as if I had just admitted to a fondness for stink bait. "It's a 10-pounder, pilgrim," he'd whisper. "But he's spooked. No use casting now."

We walked thus most of the morning, with numerous "sightings," but I did precious little casting. Gabe showed off all his expertise by pointing out numerous rises that always disappeared before I could see them.

Finally, blessedly, I was able to beg off with a vague recollection of another commitment. On the way back to the vehicles, Gabe pointed to the ground. "Moose tracks," he said. "Went through here two, maybe three, days ago." He took a few more steps and pointed again. "Elk tracks, too!" he exclaimed.

"And they're wearing horseshoes," I said. "Either that or they're both riding ponies."

Gabe was oblivious to my sarcasm because by then he had spotted a bear track. "Griz," he said, bending to examine a depression that looked to me like all the others. "Fresh. He's probably circling us."

Not 30 seconds later, we came upon a steaming pile of what was obviously horse manure. Gabe froze. "Griz for sure!" he exclaimed. "I've never seen a bigger pile of scat."

"That's horse manure," I said, and it was, too. Just like my free guide, who was worth every penny.

Compaction

❖

I lost my Diamondglass fly rod yesterday. Granted, that information will come as no small surprise to those who have also known me to lose keys, cars, and even children, but the circumstances were discombobulating, to say the least.

For one thing, the stretch of stream I was working ran along a frozen dirt road through a meadow and there was only about 100 yards of fishable water. I was presenting a scud imitation without much success when I realized I had left my fly box back at the truck. Laying the 4-weight in the grass by a basketball-size boulder, I walked 150 yards to where I had parked my vehicle, grabbed the fly box, and headed back. The rod was gone!

This can't be, I thought, mentally retracing my steps. I set the rod down here, walked over there, and walked back here. How could I not find a fly rod in such a small area? I looked about in confusion. There were other basketball-size boulders in the vicinity. Perhaps I had come back by a slightly different route to the wrong rock.

I wandered over toward another boulder. Then another. Then another yet. No fly rod. Feeling foolish, I retraced my steps nearly all the way to the truck. My stomach was beginning a rhythmic slow dance that usually becomes a frantic jitterbug when things begin to go wrong. It had started to rain. Now don't panic, I told myself. There is a very nice 4-weight out here counting on you to get it out of the elements before nightfall.

Suppressing a desire to sprint, I again went to where my rod should have been. No dice. OK, I thought, I'll do it methodically. Starting 20 feet from the water, I walked a straight line parallel to the creek, looking only to my right. When I got to the thick trees bordering the meadow, I turned and cut another 20-foot swath looking only to my left. This process I repeated until I had covered the entire area. Nothing.

Finally, it dawned on me: someone had stolen my fly rod! Someone had been watching me the whole time, and when I went to fetch the fly box he had snuck in and pilfered my Diamondglass.

Now, wait a minute, I thought. A theft out here doesn't make sense, and hadn't I suffered previously from what I call "compaction"? Mightn't this be another example of what happens when the brain gets so full with important facts, unimportant trivia, and old phone numbers there is no room left for immediate memory?

Hadn't I recently dumped dishwashing detergent in the toaster merely because I found myself standing before it with a heaping scoop? Hadn't I just showered and then walked downstairs in my altogether to do the laundry, forgetting my Aunt Judy and her husband were staying the weekend?

OK. Probably someone had *not* stolen my rod. Maybe, though, they are just hiding it. Maybe this was a joke. Maybe my fishing buddy, Steve, was hidden somewhere trying to keep from giggling. I began looking for him. "OK, buddy," I called. "That was real funny. Now let's go get a cup of coffee and call it a day." No response.

"Come on, Steve," I said. "Enough is enough. It's cold and it's starting to snow." Still no response.

When it was finally obvious to me that Steve was intent on carrying the joke too far, I trudged reluctantly back to the truck. There was my Diamondglass 4-weight in the bed, right where I had left it when I walked back to get the fly box.

Sheepishly, I climbed into the cab. I was wondering where I had put my keys.

That'll Do

❖

My daughter surprised me by setting up a new computer for me on my 60th birthday. I didn't really want a new computer, as I was just getting familiar with the old one. I would much rather have been surprised with a new drift boat.

I do not love technology, but neither did I want to lie awake all night wondering if I would be able to perform computer tasks on my new computer that most schoolchildren nail in the second grade. Therefore, I immediately sat down to write something. Better to discover deficiencies early on, I say.

Following a rather lengthy stint, I was feeling pretty good about myself, but the muscles in the back of my neck had begun to tighten. It was then I noticed the really significant difference between the new computer and my old one: this new computer was sitting much lower on my desk.

"Hey," I said to Jennifer, who had been staying busy in the background so she would be available if I became violent or caused an electrical fire with my birthday toy, "where's my fly-tying book?"

"Fly-tying book?" Jennifer questioned. "I haven't seen any fly-tying book."

"You must have," I insisted. "It's called *Creative Tying: Designing Flies with Stuff Found Around the House*. It was 3 inches thick, and I used it to raise my monitor to a comfortable height. Remember? I put it up there when I got that tickling sensation in my neck four years ago. It made the monitor just the right height so the nerves in my neck weren't getting pinched when I wrote my fly-fishing columns."

"Oh, that book," Jennifer said. "Dad, that book made your whole desk look tacky. A man who makes his living with his computer should not have a book like that under his monitor to make it the proper height."

"Would *Great Rivers/Great Hatches* be better?" I asked. "It may not be thick enough, though. And it wouldn't be very handy under my monitor; I refer to it a lot."

Jennifer sputtered and left the room mumbling something about bubble gum and baling wire. My knack for making things serviceable with a minimum of expense and no expertise drives her a little crazy.

On assorted fishing trips, I have employed rubber bands, paper clips, metal ink cartridges, superglue, and assorted sticks to get my gear back in working order, but bubble gum has always been one of my favorites. With a big wad of Bazooka I have patched leaky rowboats and waders and even fixed the drag on a broken reel. Bubble gum has been there when I needed to keep an obstinate fly box closed or retrieve a fly dropped between boulders on Penns Creek.

Baling wire is my other favorite fix-it thing, and I am saddened that more and more farmers are putting up their hay with that orange plastic twine that doesn't even make a good knot. Over the years, I have used baling wire to hold down a truck canopy, help trailer a boat, pick a motel lock (it was my motel, but the key was somewhere in the Sand River), and mount a fly reel. I've cooked small trout on a baling wire skewer, and when I was a kid, baling wire made a great stringer.

Obviously, despite my preferences, neither bubble gum nor baling wire would work to bring my monitor up to the right height. After Jennifer gave up on me, though, I found something to set it on that would work just as well: an antique tackle box full of old marlin flies. The prominence of such a low-tech item in my new high-tech office pleases me greatly.

Yellow Jacket Safari

———✦✧✦———

I don't mind most bugs. As a creator of assorted strange fly patterns, I use insects as my models. Beetles, I think, are particularly cool. You can turn a beetle on its back, and he will stay there all day, treading air and wishing he had put on his sneakers for better traction. Trout love beetle imitations that do this.

When I taught a middle school entomology unit, my students were required to put together bug collections. They brought in the usual bees and ants and moths, and when the unit was finally over they would all try their hand at tying a fly to match a bug in their collection. Then we would go fishing.

Part of my students' final grade each year was based on "tasteful presentation" (if that is possible with a piece of cardboard covered with dead things). The only insect I didn't require to be displayed in tasteful, terminal condition were yellow jackets. I like my yellow jackets squished.

I despise yellow jackets. They are the only insects I know of that are mean for the sake of being mean. If a common honeybee lands on your arm, she will stroll around a little, decide you are the wrong flavor and consistency, and buzz off. Both psychotic and homicidal, yellow jackets will sting you as an afterthought. It's like "Oh yeah—I forgot something. Have a taste of my stinger, sucker!"

It used to be that when my family camped, we would hang a hot dog above a pail of soapy water. In theory, the yellow jackets would gorge until they were so full they fell in the water. In actuality, most of them ate their fill, washed up, and then flew home to get the kids.

The most satisfying yellow jacket purge I have ever participated in took place this past summer. Sitting at a picnic table after a day of throwing streamers at browns, trying to enjoy a slice of watermelon from my cooler, I was suddenly swarmed by yellow-and-black thieves set on eating my treat and doing me bodily harm.

In the beginning, I did the usual frantic swatting and cursing, but then I remembered the can of flying-insect spray in the car. I returned with it to the table, popped the lid, and cut loose. The first squirt took out four yellow jackets that writhed very satisfactorily before expiring in a puddle of pink watermelon juice.

The second blast netted me three more of the tenacious beasts. Then—an inspiration! I took the seven carcasses and arranged them around the outside of the plate as decoys.

In singles and pairs, more yellow jackets came to my decoy spread. After a time, they began circling warily, but I adjusted my lead and took them from midair. Applying the same principles as in wing-shooting mallards, I took lefts and rights and even some tricky overheads.

I was having so much fun that, when it got too dark to calculate lead and velocity, I turned on the car headlights, but by then the survivors had given up and big, white moths were circling crazily. I took out a few of them also. But moths are too easy, and I began to feel guilty.

That night, I thought about middle school bug collections and pondered the delightful possibility of repeating the day's shooting performance at the river using "decoys" of my own creation—hand-tied yellow jacket imitations that would turn every summer outing into a "cast and blast." I felt a lot better about yellow jackets when I finally drifted off.

Dressing Alan

❖

Mike and I have been fly fishing together for 30 years; we're very good friends. He hadn't realized how close we'd become, however, until a recent fishing trip to Colorado's Roaring Fork River.

The day before, we'd hit it hard in the rain, trying to find a soft spot on the unyielding wooden seats of our McKenzie boat. Cold and stiff at day's end, we'd then slept on camper beds that were too short, too hard, and too cold. For Mike, that wasn't a problem. He is short and thin and has a job with UPS that keeps him in shape. I am tall and overweight and spend many hours each day warring with pop-ups on my computer screen.

We were supposed to meet a new friend and guide, Gary, in a few minutes, but when I awoke at 5 a.m. I knew there were going to be problems—my back was out.

"Darling," I called from the upper berth over the cab, "are you awake?"

My friend grunted. He was sleeping below me, where the table had been disassembled to make a second bed.

"Darling," I repeated, "are you awake?"

Mike stirred, but he still didn't say anything for a long time. Finally, his hesitant voice broke the silence. "Am I 'darling?' " he asked timidly. There was another long pause, then, "What do you want?"

"I have to use the bathroom," I said.

Judging by the lack of response, Mike was evidently processing this information carefully. "We don't have a bathroom," he said at last. "Go outside."

I attempted again to rise, but an electric-like shock in my lower back slammed me to the mattress. "I was going to," I said through clenched teeth, "but there's a problem. Can you help me?"

"I don't think that's in the Buddy Manual," Mike said. "Quitcher screwin' around."

"Mike!" I persisted. "Just help me put my pants on so I can go outside." I wormed around enough to get on my side, where I could peer down at my friend, who had his bag pulled up to his nose. The whites of his eyes were all I could see. When he noticed me staring at him, he pretended to be asleep again.

Finally, reluctantly, Mike threw back his sleeping bag and rolled onto the floor. He grabbed my jeans from atop the camper refrigerator, where I had carefully wadded them.

"Try to slip them over my feet so I can pull them up," I said. "If you can get them to my knees, I can do the rest."

Standing beside my bed, Mike attempted to do what I had instructed. "Your big toe is hanging up," he grunted. "Have you ever considered cutting your toenails?"

"Maybe you'd like to do that for me, too," I said.

"I don't think so," he replied. He stopped to assess the situation a minute, then crawled up onto the foot of the bed with me. Pushing, pulling, grunting, the camper swaying with the exertion, he wrestled the jeans as far as my calves.

He was leaning over me, pulling mightily, when the door opened and Gary popped his head in. "Rise and shine!" he started to say, but he only got as far as the second word. His mouth dropped open. "Oh! Am I interrupting something?"

"Not much," Mike replied. "You wanna try this?"

"I'm trying to quit," Gary said. "Why don't you guys just meet me at the river?"

Ten minutes later, Mike and I walked down to meet Gary, but he wasn't there, and though we waited an hour, he never did show up. I've phoned and left several messages since, but he has never returned my call. Now tell me—what kind of guide is that?

The Ling in My Sink

❦

When I was in my 20s, two friends and I would drive up to Kootenay Lake in British Columbia and fish for freshwater lingcod. The ling is an odd, catfish-looking creature, also known as a burbot. In Kootenay, it grew big, and with the generous 15-fish limit of the time, three of us would often come back to the dock with 300 pounds of fish. Sometimes we'd do so three nights in a row.

It was impossible to eat that much fish before it went bad in the freezer, but even when British Columbia finally wised up and reduced the limit, it was still too generous. Today there are so few ling in Kootenay Lake the season has been suspended.

I imagine dams and droughts and a lot of other factors led to the decimation of the Kootenay Lake lingcod, but I can't help but think my friends and I were also responsible. That's one of the reasons I'm now in my "compensation phase" of angling, trying to atone for some of the atrocities of my youth. That's why I mostly fly fish. Oh, I still keep enough fillets for a meal now and then, but I let most of my fish go. The ling in my sink, however, is proof I have not perfected catch-and-release.

The ling in my sink is 2 feet long. It is curled around the drain plug in 10 inches of water, and I'm not quite sure what it is doing there. If my 8-year-old nephew comes over, I'll tell him it swam up through the drainpipe. Uncles are supposed to say stuff like that, and it would be a lot easier than the truth, which is yet to be sorted out.

I was bumping a weighted white fly along the bottom of the Kettle River, prospecting for whitefish, when I caught the ling— the first I'd ever seen outside Kootenay Lake. I figured it weighed but a couple of pounds, but I'd had no other success that day, and it looked to me like even at 2 pounds there were a couple decent fillets. I threw it in the cooler.

At home nine hours later, I prepared to clean my catch. It was still alive! On a whim, I put it in the sink and filled the sink with water. Now it has righted itself, its gills are working, and it is exploring its stainless steel confines.

What a beautiful thing this fish is. The markings on its back and sides are leopard-like, much like the green-and-brown paisley tie I wore in the '70s. I never really looked at all those fish I killed at Kootenay Lake 30 years ago. Caught at night, killed, and kept on ice, they weren't cleaned until morning. They were washed-out and stiff when we got to them, covered with death slime—no more than fodder for a fish fry.

The ling has become more active in the sink. I prod it gently with a finger and touch the barbels under its chin, charmed by its eel-like qualities. What will I do with a ling in my sink? I can either clean it or release it, but at midnight in Spokane, Washington, there is really no place to release a lingcod.

To me, the choice is logical. I lift the squirming fish from the water and carry it to the bathroom. I put it gently in the tub and fill the tub with cold water. In the morning, I will drive 70 miles back to the Kettle River and let it go: compensation. Hopefully, no one will see me.

The Liere Chronicles

———— ⟋⟍⟍ ————

A fellow fly fisherman who is also a prominent Spokane psychologist stepped into my office the other day. "Jeez, Liere," he said, looking around. "I need to spend some time in here. This is not the workplace of a normal man."

To me, my office seems pretty normal. On one desk are a computer, a printer, and a scanner. On another are a stack of 35 mm slides and a viewing box. A fax machine sits atop a metal two-drawer file cabinet, and my shelves are crammed with reference books, brochures, and binders.

Oh, sure, there are a few mounted fish, including a 27-pound laker that seems to be swimming through the room, attached to the ceiling with 12-pound monofilament. The office also holds a gold pan, lots of fish pictures, a homemade sign that says "BORN TO FISH; FORCED TO WORK," a Civil War sword, a beaver hide, an antiquated Zenith radio, and a stuffed rattlesnake.

But the angler/psychologist wasn't particularly interested in those things. He was staring at the file cabinet next to the closet door, the one where I keep the single bowling trophy and the picture of my daughter in her junior high basketball uniform—which are surrounded by a diverse collection of odds and ends I've picked up over the years, deemed worthwhile, and kept.

Once home with these treasures, I found I really had no place for them. Or perhaps that was just my excuse to keep them near at hand. I tossed them on the file cabinet, promising myself I would deal with them later. The top of the file cabinet is only 18 inches by 28 inches. It is amazing that I have crammed so many items into such a small area.

A barnacle-encrusted Crown Royal bottle is up there—a reminder of a spring vacation on Barkley Sound, where I caught my first rock bass on a fly. Close by are a moose tooth I found while fishing for grayling in Alaska, a thumb brace that got me through the winter steelhead season, and a king salmon tail that measures 14 inches from tip to tip. Yup—caught it on a fly.

There are several worn-out fly reels on my file cabinet—all with a story—and also a rusty 10-penny nail, a wild turkey egg, a Franz Dutzler brook trout carving, and a half-used bottle of trombone slide oil that belonged to my father. There is a plastic film canister holding both the "spur" from an African spurwing goose and the big, ragged streamer that fooled a sheefish in Alaska.

An old faucet from my first house, a jar of rocks, a waterbed repair kit, a J.C. Higgins level-wind fishing reel, an old Johnson Citation spin-casting reel, nine gold-foil-covered chocolate "coins," and a coffee mug from the first restaurant in Coulee City, Washington, also adorn my file cabinet. In the mug are a bottle of fly dressing and a book of matches. An 11-inch turkey beard is there, too, as is a blue pin-on button that says "CONTEST WINNER" and my most recent addition—the small yellow tags I took from the backs of the two Lake Roosevelt trout we had for dinner last night.

"What will you do with all this stuff?" my wife asked me this morning. She was in a cleaning frenzy, but, as always, the awesome mess in my office had knocked the wind from her sails.

"What stuff?" I asked her.

"The stuff on your file," she said.

"You mean 'The Liere Chronicles'?" I asked. "My life diary? What would I do without it?" Then, as always, I smiled. "Don't worry, dear," I said. "I'll deal with it later."

Demon Jim Beam

Recently, I wrote a letter of apology to a rancher near Three Rivers, Montana. I doubt if he even remembered me, but I didn't want to take a chance, because he had some really nice cutthroat in the creek meandering through his property. I'd like to be invited back to fish.

After finally tracking him down one evening last August to seek permission to trespass, a friend and I sat at this fellow's kitchen table and, while the friend politely sipped on two beers, the rancher and I consumed a prodigious quantity of the rancher's bourbon. It didn't seem to bother him any, but for me it was really dumb, because I hadn't eaten all day and, when it comes to liquor of any sort, I'm what my friend calls a "lightweight."

This designation began during my formative youth, when, on a dare, I chugged a bottle of Annie Green Springs one rainy October evening prior to a college dance. Not only did I miss the dance, I got sick on the front porch of the college librarian. For some reason, I got it in my head that she could help me find my misplaced shoes, but shortly after ringing her doorbell I treated her to a look at the spaghetti I'd had for dinner and she called the campus police.

I was pretty sure my mother wouldn't like it when she heard I was in the pokey, so I hid under a nearby car. This wasn't a real good idea either, because the car had merely stopped for a light, and when the light turned green I was pretty much just lying there on the wet asphalt thinking I would die and wondering why I hadn't.

Though my condition by the end of the evening in Montana seemed to tickle the rancher, my friend said he thought the fellow was getting tired of my sheep jokes and that I shouldn't have scared his young daughter by pretending to pull off my thumb. I later wished with all my heart that the bottle of Jim Beam had been a pint rather than a half gallon, for I had three evil forces working against me that evening. One was my aforementioned intolerance for firewater; another was the fact that I wanted to come off as a congenial good old boy. It has been my observation that good ol' boys get permission to fish private land more readily than do I; my Southern friends call me "a Yankee bluenose." Good ol' boys know how to bend their elbows.

The third force working against me that night was that my friend had introduced me as an outdoor writer. For some reason, people expect outdoor writers to be hard-drinkin' men-about-town. I think Ernest Hemingway and Robert Ruark contributed strongly to this perception. With that in mind, I just didn't feel it would be appropriate for me to ask for an iced tea with artificial sweetener and a twist of lemon, which was what really sounded good at the time.

We did manage to secure permission to fish the fellow's ranch, but the next day my head and stomach couldn't keep up with my desire to drop a size-14 mosquito imitation on the nose of an 18-inch cutthroat. I spent the morning moaning in the backseat of the car while my friend had take after take, releasing some beauties and returning with five smaller trout for dinner. I don't recall ever being quite so miserable outside of college, but permission to fish a good piece of cutthroat water is hard to come by, and my friend tells me my battle with demon Jim Beam was well worth the misery. Easy for him to say.

Ugly Weather

A s I write this on the first of July, black clouds scud low and ominous over the top of Pease Mountain, and though I can't see the misty rain through my dirty windows, the dimples on the wet slab in front of the garage confirm its presence. I am profoundly affected by unseasonal weather, and my mood is as dark as the sky.

I should be wandering Sand Creek with a fly rod, looking for a hungry brown trout. But even with my "space age" rain gear, today I am not particularly motivated to slosh about in the high grass. I have always thought fly fishing more sensible than golf, but in weather like this—so contrary to expectations—nothing seems to make much sense. Funny—in December, I will wade Demon Creek in a sleet storm and love every minute of it, but in summer, when it's supposed to be sunshine, lollipops, and caddisfly hatches, I am extremely intolerant of the gloom. Today, the adrenaline rush of fooling a big brown is not as appealing as just being on the river on a glorious summer morning, and there haven't been many of those this year. I have yet to nod off in the afternoon sun while leaning against a smooth streamside blowdown after changing patterns. That just isn't right.

This morning I tried to read a fishing book in front of the fire, but the book wasn't very good, and neither was my fire, and the act of building it put me in a funk. This is the time to be cutting wood for next year, not burning what remains of the skimpy stash. One should not have to crank up the woodstove in the middle of summer.

Despite these opinions, I know ugly weather is in the eye of the beholder. In a perfect world, the weather would always cooperate with me. All I really want are a few typical Saturdays for each season, so I can plan my fishing trips and adjust my attitude and clothing to the weather. That would mean cold winters, sparkling springs, hot, lazy summers, and crisp, dry autumns—except when I am duck hunting.

Folks attending a high school football game would probably prefer what duck hunters sadly call "a bluebird day"—bright sun in a cloudless sky. I must admit I have no affection for rain and wind if I am watching gridiron goings-on from the bleachers, and I cherish the bluebird days of September and October when I am plying the Mighty Mo for big browns.

I'm very flexible in November, December, and January—almost complacent about my lot, though at least one prolonged freeze would be nice for putting a cap on area lakes. I dearly love to cast a white fly for whitefish on a partially frozen river. Friends suggest that what I really dearly love is to leave the river for the comfort of a roaring car heater and a shot of homemade blueberry hooch. Friends are perceptive, though smoked whitefish are really quite delectable.

February and March have traditionally been dreary, but I can live with dreary if I can get on the water a few times. For me, February and March are about anticipation as much as anything. They are like liver—one must partake of the bad so that one might appreciate a T-bone. After that, I'm back to April and May and a new beginning. Then it's summer again, hopefully with summer-like weather—my favorite time to fish. I'm really looking forward to casting Yellow Sallies into the deep pools on Sand Creek. I also hope that big blowdown wasn't washed away in the spring torrent.

These Old Bones

For me, the biggest event of the year was my 60th birthday party. Boy, was I glad to finally reach that milestone! At last, I have a reason to feel as bad as I do after fly fishing all day. Oh, I'm not ready for the boneyard yet, mind you, but I've certainly got my share of infirmities.

My father used to say that aches and pains were the proof of a life honestly lived. My mom, however, wasn't buying into it. "Walt," she'd say in her gentle, sympathetic way, "shut up! There's nothing honest about getting kicked by a pack mule."

When I was in high school, I played football and basketball, one contributing a broken nose and a bum knee, the other a torn Achilles tendon and bone spurs. Seems I was not the stuff of NFL or NBA legends, though I did set a record for projectile vomiting at halftime of a particularly tense basketball game against our crosstown rival.

Now, the morning after a day spent stumbling over rounded river rock or paddling a float tube 12 miles in 36-degree water, I lie in bed wondering where the cheerleaders are, wondering why I once forsook so many fishing opportunities and abused my youthful body merely for the pleasure of getting sweaty and tired on Friday nights in a high school gymnasium.

In all fairness, I must say that high school sports alone are not responsible for the shape I'm in. No, I must also lay some of the blame on college. I discovered Sloe Gin Fizzes in college, abused the drink terribly, and am now paying the consequences.

The ache in my casting arm? An inebriated wrestling match in my apartment that sent my roommate and I over the couch, separating my shoulder. The achy hip? A Fizz-induced sledding accident. The fact is, nothing good ever happened in my life because of alcohol, unless you count the night Billy Bunwad quit being my friend because I told him if he didn't stop bugging my sister I'd rip his heart out and eat it.

One good thing about having so many medical afflictions is it gives me something to talk about with my friends, and it's also an excuse for just missing that rise midriver. I remember when a bunch of us guys would get together in fish camp and talk about nothing but fly fishing and women. Now, most of them talk about Lotrel and Zocor, prostates and angiograms.

When I visit assorted friends and relatives in assorted nursing homes and assisted-living facilities, I am able to communicate in a way I never dreamed possible. Heck yes, I think calcium supplements cause kidney stones. No, I never did try Mercurochrome for toenail fungus, but those chemical heat packs really help lower back pain.

I still get out and do a lot of fly fishing every year, but I pay for it terribly afterward. Last week, I stalked browns on Wilson Creek. I felt pretty good when I quit for the day, but by the time I got home, I couldn't get out of the truck by myself. Eventually, I took a Vioxx and slipped into the hot tub. Oh, I know—it has been decided that Vioxx causes all sorts of heart and blood problems. But sometimes, if you want to go fishing badly enough, the possible consequences seem a small risk to take. In fact, if you have any Vioxx you want to dispose of, I'd be happy to pick it up.

Getting a Hair

❖

In January, I decided to refinish my 4-weight bamboo rod. This was not a well-considered determination, but rather something my father used to call "getting a hair." According to him, I got a hair quite often during my formative years—quick, decisive decisions based on absolutely nothing but impulse. Usually, the consequences of "getting a hair" were less than impressive.

I got a hair once in college and decided to take a fall quarter off to continue my summer job with the Forest Service in north Idaho. Actually, I was more interested in challenging the cutthroat in Kalispell Creek than working, but the decision immediately changed my draft status from that of student to that of potential infantryman.

When I took my pre-induction physical, however, it was determined that I had the auditory discrimination of a turnip—the result of another "hair" during my youth when I decided a metal machine shed would be an excellent place to touch off a thousand firecrackers. The Army didn't want me so I went back to school, where I distinguished myself academically by graduating in six years with a 2.13 grade point average, having many hairs along the way.

But back to my most recent hair—my bamboo 4-weight. It didn't really need refinishing; I just decided it was something I wanted to do, and a friend had given me a video showing how it was done. Having always relied on my children to mess with the VCR, and having no children at home when I got the hair, I promptly caused the entire system to malfunction—including the TV. With football playoffs in progress that afternoon, this was not an inconsequential consideration.

I drove to a local sports bar to watch the games, but after six hours of back-to-backs on Saturday, I needed a cab ride home. That is the thing I hate most about sports bars: you feel obligated to eat and drink too much while you are there to show your appreciation to the nice proprietor who is letting you watch his TV.

The next day, I called a friend to pick me up so I could retrieve my truck, promising to buy him breakfast for his trouble. During the meal, someone sideswiped my truck in the parking lot, putting a crease in the driver's door. I called my insurance agent, who immediately made arrangements for me to meet with an adjuster, but on the way I slid off the road and through a fence, effectively hiding the crease on the door with a bigger crease.

Again I called my insurance agent, and this time he said he'd send the adjuster to me. The sheriff got there before the adjuster, though, and tried to give me a ticket for driving too fast for the conditions. I told him I had been going less than 20 miles per hour and refused to take the ticket. I told him anyone could see that, had I been going too fast, my truck would have rolled much farther once it went through the fence.

The sheriff put me in the back of his car and told me to calm down. I told him I had not even started on my fly rod and already it had cost me my thousand-dollar deductible. The sheriff seemed puzzled. He also gave me the ticket.

Now I'm supposed to hire a counselor at $100 an hour and do some anger management work—all because I decided to refinish my 4-weight. See what I mean about the consequences of getting a hair?

The Scabs on My Head

◆

There's a scab on the top of my head. It's been there since 1962. Most of my older friends don't mention it anymore, and more recent acquaintances assume that because it never goes away it is a birthmark.

The fact is, in 1962 I grew 3 inches, which made me 6 feet, 4 inches tall. At 6 feet, 1 inch there had been no real problems in my life, unless you count Charlene Bereiter or athlete's foot, but at 6 feet, 4 inches I started hitting things with the top of my head. Crawl spaces and attics and truck campers that had once treated me with indifference ganged up to gouge skin and hair from my unsuspecting noggin. Low-slung tree branches joined the assault, and cupboard doors got in their licks, too.

The only difference between then and now, though, is that in 1962 I still had 4 pounds of hair; today I have little. An accumulation of scrapes and bad genes has reduced my dark, curly mop to a rather barren acre garnished for humorous affect with six longish, lonesome hairs. Every new crease in my head is on display.

Last summer in Alaska is an example. Five friends and I rented a 26-foot motor home in Soldotna and headed out for a week of salmon fishing. We knew there were places on the Kenai and the Russian where a fly fisherman could wear himself out catching fish.

Early on, it became apparent the doorjambs of our motor home would accommodate only about 6 feet 3½ inches of a 6-foot 4-inch man. The other half inch, unless that man remembers to duck, is gradually scraped off against the upper molding.

The motor home also had a skylight in the ceiling of the kitchen tastefully trimmed with oak, which made it just a hair and some skin too low for me to pass under comfortably.

To hide my wounds, I took to wearing a baseball cap. Its presence on my head initially tempered a great deal of the flak I was getting from my friends, but it did nothing to stop the carnage. In fact, it seemed that, as the week progressed, I was gouging my head in places I had once passed beneath safely. Obviously, I was getting taller.

I took to stuffing toilet paper under my cap to cushion the inevitable collisions, a stratagem that made me the butt of sniggers from other anglers on Bird Creek when one of the little pieces of white tissue snaked from underneath and flopped in the wind like a crepe-paper banner.

On the second-to-last day of the trip, Ron Daisy, who is the same height as I, solved the mystery of my perpetually bleeding noggin. He was sitting next to me in the kitchen, tying up a bunch of red-and-white sockeye streamers, and quite obviously bemused by the multiple toilet-paper flags again projecting from beneath my cap.

"Do you by any chance notice anything different between the top of my head and the top of yours?" he asked.

"Very funny," I said.

"It's the little metal button on top of your hat," he said. "It's just high enough to hit the ceiling. Every time you stand up, it hits the ceiling and pushes down into the top of your head."

"Come on!" I said defensively. "You think I'm gonna let something like that happen? Jeez, man, that would be really dumb. Give me some credit."

Nevertheless, I immediately quit wearing the cap, and when I got back home my wounds were healing. I still measured 6 feet, 4 inches, too—unless you added the scabs, which stuck up there quite a ways.

Ice-Fishing Magic

———◦∾∾◦———

I know, I know—fly fishing is best, but a lot of rivers are closed during the winter months, and even if they're not, the trout aren't exactly jumping out of their scales to take your beaded nymph. Don't you think ice fishing would be OK once in a while?

I truly believe there is an element of magic to ice fishing. Those who have never considered the entertainment and meditative value inherent in staring wistfully into a hole augered through frozen water say I am not only daft but a traitor for thinking this, but it is true. If I can't be fly fishing, no other winter activity allows me so much enjoyment for so little effort.

In May and June, I expect to catch fish because I can pick my fly and my spot with a careful eye to weather, structure, temperature, and time of day. When I am dunking a maggot-tipped Swedish Pimple through a 6-inch ice hole in late winter, however, there is more chance involved.

Besides persistence and the fact that God watches over fools and small children, there is no reason why I should catch fish through the ice. One hole, after all, looks the same as another, and everyone uses virtually the same thing and fishes the same acre of lake. There are 628 other acres out there where the fish can feed.

Hopefully, an 8-inch perch will eventually come twisting up out of the darkness to wriggle beside the hole I have drilled, the fish's shimmering colors enhanced by its contrast to the ice. That's part of the magic, this sudden emergence into the light, and my joy exceeds by far the simplicity of the act.

Some days, fish by the dozens are taken from only three or four holes, and the rest of the frozen-nose brigade might just as well have augered through the 2 feet of snow in their backyards. Some will go home, but most will pick up and wander, eyes down, along an apparent haphazard path, studying cracks and bumps in the ice as if they have inside information concerning the correlation between icy structure and fishy hangouts. Magically, they'll soon find themselves 10 feet from the hot hole. "Doing any good?" they ask innocently as they take up their auger and begin to drill.

Oddly, I like ice fishing even when there are no fish. Television bores me, but I can watch a tiny sponge bobber for hours, tensed for the telltale nervousness of water that says a perch has nudged my offering and may have other, greater intentions. If it doesn't, though, that's OK. On the ice, I go inside myself for both entertainment and warmth, and I have found I care for my company and my opinions a great deal.

"Beats sittin' at home" is a refrain you hear often when ice fishing. It's as if we fly anglers must apologize for our insanity, justify our presence on frozen water when the temperature is in the low teens and more civilized people are lounging before a warm fire with a mug of Starbucks and a copy of *Trout Bum*.

"There's nothing wrong with a little vicarious adventure on a cold day," my wife reminds me as I pull on my long underwear. She likes to fish, but not in the winter. "Right," I say. "I'll be back after dark. I want to catch the evening bite."

"Have a good time, then." She smiles sincerely and goes back to her book. No hassle, no guilt. Pure magic.

Driving 299

❖❖❖

Having already wandered way too many miles as I fished my way through central Oregon last summer, I was planning on breezing through to my son's house in Eureka, California, on a decent, direct route. We were going to spend a few days fly fishing some of the excellent trout waters near his home.

On a road map, the 135 miles of California Highway 299 between Redding and Eureka looked as if it should take just over two hours to drive. I was looking forward to a quick last leg, possibly fast enough to get me to my son's place in time for dinner.

No such luck. Right away, Highway 299 began to wind uphill, with speed limits ranging from 35 to 45 miles per hour unless you're behind a trailer; I was behind a trailer. The California Highway Department, anticipating such slow-moving vehicles, had thoughtfully placed a series of turnouts every 10 miles or so. This is a wonderful concept if the slow vehicles in front of you are inclined to use them. The one in front of me wasn't.

I waited for a passing lane, but passing lanes, unfortunately, are always on hills. On hills, with my diesel truck carrying a heavy camper, I became the "passee" rather than the passer. With a string of cars riding my bumper, I had no polite choice but to stay behind the trailer.

After two hours, I was still 60 miles from Eureka when the white trailer pulled into a rest stop and I triumphantly swept by. My elation was soon tempered, however, by the realization that I should have pulled into the rest stop too; my 16-ounce Pepsi was taking up way too much room. Not wanting to relinquish my position, I kept driving.

I was going to explode! In desperation, I hit upon a plan for relieving myself on the fly, using the empty Pepsi container. Through a rather intricate maneuver while driving a windy, hilly road at 40 mph, I nevertheless had accomplished the initial formalities when I rounded a sharp curve and was confronted by a road construction crew and a flagman, who in this case was a flagwoman.

Clenching the bottle to my nether regions and attempting to stifle the flow as she approached the window, I was not in the mood for conversation.

"Hi," she said cheerfully. "You just missed the pilot car. There will be a 10-minute delay."

"OK," I growled. I was hoping my frown would send her looking for a friendlier tourist behind me.

"Where you from?" she asked.

"North," I said. I felt somewhat like an exhibitionist speaking to this young lady while holding an intimate part of me to the mouth of a Pepsi container. I was praying she wouldn't get any closer to the window.

Finally, after a little more small talk, she left me to go visit with the couple in the vehicle behind me, and I was able to release my grip, watching in horror as urine rose precariously higher in the bottle. Obviously, my bladder had been holding back much more than 16 ounces of Pepsi.

When the pilot car finally returned, I pretty much had a mess on my hands . . . and my pants . . . and my shoes . . . and the seat of my truck. Soon after the pilot car released me, I pulled over at a turnout and went inside my camper to clean up. I came out just in time to see the white trailer go by. I wondered if I'd be in Eureka in time to catch the early caddisfly hatch the next morning.

Fire!

U ntil the discovery of fire, I assume cavemen and cave
women ate their steaks very rare, probably without A-1
or even salt. Good enough that it had temporarily quit
squirming. The first medium-rare steak was probably carved from
an unlucky mastodon that couldn't outrun a lightning-caused
conflagration.

After that first epicurean breakthrough, primitive man most
likely carried his fire with him, though how he managed it without
wheels for his Weber is beyond me. Eventually, he learned how to
get a good blaze going with flint and tinder, or by rubbing sticks
together.

Until my wife and I fished Alaska for two weeks in the early
'90s, I had always thought much ado was made of the process of
building a campfire—the right kind of wood, the right kindling
arrangement, the right kind of rocks in the fire pit. Basically, when
I wanted a campfire, I wadded up some newspapers, tossed on a
couple of pinecones, and lit a match.

In Alaska, Lacey and I discovered that making a campfire was
a far greater challenge than we'd ever experienced closer to home.
Wood was in short supply, and dry wood was almost nonexistent.
Campgrounds along the Kenai River where we landed the first
night had been so thoroughly gleaned by campers desperate for
cheery warmth that it was impossible to find wood of any sort.
Finally, we stumbled upon an old pallet lying along the river. Our
romantic campfire was salvaged! We dragged it back to camp, and
though it was very wet, I doused it with gasoline, made a gasoline
trail, and applied my Bic. The event was documented by the Sterling
Volunteer Fire Department, which was called, rather prematurely, I
thought, by some campers 400 yards down the river who thought
a plane had crashed.

All in all, it was a bit of an embarrassment, and for the next two weeks I started smudges the old-fashioned way: with a stack of newspapers, carefully shaved wood splinters, a couple of boxes of wooden matches, and quite a bit of swearing. Near the end of our stay, however, Lacey and I spent a particularly long day drifting red-and-white streamer flies for coho salmon in a steady drizzle. Then, because we needed to get closer to Haines, where we would be catching a ferry to Prince Rupert the next morning, we drove two hours, finally finding a private campground with one space available. It had an elaborate barbecue pit with a grate and a stovepipe. A fire was our first priority.

I was not in the mood for fighting with wet wood. I crammed the fire pit with birch and dumped on about a half gallon of gas. "Stand back, dear," I said, and touched it off.

The sound it made was very much like that of an F-16 on a strafing run. WHOOSH! does not do it justice, because WHOOSH has a soft ending. It's more like a WHOOOOM! that reverberates several minutes.

A half gallon of gas going up a stovepipe can shoot flames 25 feet in the air, bring all nearby campers stumbling from their tents, and make small children cry. The chaos lasted many minutes, and afterwards Lacey would not speak to me, even though I was in pain.

The next day, she emptied all the gasoline from our emergency can into the truck. She also hid the matches and then borrowed and "lost" my Bic. She needn't have worried, though, that I'd ever revert to my Alaska method of fire starting. Burn off your eyebrows just once and you'll understand why.

The Glue That Binds

—〰—

On the first warm day in May, I walked to the end of a rickety Tater Lake dock to cast for crappie. Crappie are excellent competitors against a 4-weight fly rod, and they are good for you, too—high in all the healthy stuff, low in all the unhealthy stuff. The healthy stuff cancels out the Twinkies, Cheetos, Mountain Dew, and other worthless calories I consume while I am fishing for crappie in the spring.

Right off the bat, I got a size-16 black marabou fly hooked in my trouser cuff. Attempting to remove it with a fillet knife, I somehow managed to put a deep, gaping, 2-inch wound on the knuckle side of the middle finger on my left hand. Pressing the wound closed, I raised both hands above my head to slow the blood flow. Then I walked back to my car where I wrapped an old wool glove tightly around the wound. Positioning the glove so I could hold it in place with the thumb of the bleeding hand, I drove to a convenience store down the lake where I bought tape and gauze.

Outside in the parking lot, I tended my wound, but I couldn't cut the tape or gauze, and when I finished, my finger was only slightly smaller than an Egyptian mummy. As an afterthought, I went back in the store and purchased a tube of Super Glue. I had read that doctors sometimes use Super Glue instead of sutures to close a wound.

I returned to the lake to retrieve my rod, but in the process, the wound reopened. No matter what I did, the finger would not stop bleeding. If I kept it raised, the flow slowed considerably, but when I brought it down to where I could get a good look, blood poured from beneath the dressing. Not wanting to drive back to the motel until the blood had stopped running, I removed the mummy while holding the finger above my head, brought it down quickly, squeezed on half the tube of Super Glue, pinched the wound shut with my other hand, and then rested both hands on top of my head . . . where they became stuck.

In times of great embarrassment, physical pain is inconsequential. An example would be the day I ripped my tongue from a frozen bus stop sign when I saw my third-grade heartthrob, Loreen, coming up the street. My present predicament with the Super Glue was another example. I knew I needed to ask for help. It was bad enough, though, that I had a bloody, Super Glued digit and that my hands were stuck together. I absolutely could not bear the thought of someone seeing me with my hands glued to the top of my head.

I counted to three, squeezed my eyes shut, and jerked. The pain was intense, but I was able to bring my connected hands and about half my scalp down in front of my body. I would have left then, but driving a stick shift would have been a tricky proposition with my hands glued together.

I walked to the nearest house and knocked on the door with my elbow. An older gentleman answered. When I explained my predicament and he quit rolling on the floor, he invited me in and used some solvent to get my hands apart. He took a look at my finger and said he thought it looked pretty good.

"Nasty scalp wound, though," he observed.

"I've had worse," I said. "You ever had your tongue stuck to a frozen bus sign?"

I Hear You Now (Sometimes)

$\Diamond$

OK, I finally got a cell phone. Now I too can be contacted by people I do not want to talk to, at times and in places I do not want to talk.

Oh, wait—there is one difference: I have given no one my number, and just to be on the safe side, I take my phone with me only if I know I must make a business call at 10 a.m.—the same time I plan to be casting leech patterns for Stone Creek browns.

"But what if there's an emergency on the way to the river?" I am asked by incredulous acquaintances. "What if you break down on a lonely back road in the middle of a snow storm? You've got to have your cell phone with you!"

"I've met a lot of really fine people during life-threatening situations," I tell them. "I think it is beautiful how adversity binds humanity. And what good is life if it is always safe, sterile, and predictable? How can there be an adventure without risk, and how can there be risk with cell phones?"

Okay, that verbiage is admittedly too eloquent for me. What I actually do is gently suggest they go to hell.

I use my cell phone for business, and to tell the truth, I feel deliciously naughty to be engaged in a business-related discussion while sitting on a streamside stump, watching mayflies mate.

If I do have my phone with me, and it rings, I don't answer. It's actually pretty simple, though I know it is mind-boggling to those who will sacrifice any number of body parts to get to a ringing phone.

Remember how little kids say, "Me do"? It is an innate human tendency to take responsibility for your own actions. In some ways, a cell phone circumvents this process by making mom or dad or grandpa—security—just a ring away. My friend Lester has not figured this out. Lester calls his out-of-state children and grandchildren every morning now that he has a cell phone. He makes me want to mangle his antenna, especially when we are on a fishing trip and he is calling from a tent camp or a motel room and getting all animated, talking fishing and baby talk and trying to solve everyone's problems.

"Why do you do that, Lester?" I asked him once.

"It's cheap," was his answer.

"Well, what would happen if you didn't call every morning?" I asked. "What if everyone had to wait until we got home to hear about our fine fish and flawless presentations, and to get your opinion of cotton versus flannel sheets for the crib?"

Lester had to think about that one for a while. "I guess I wouldn't be saving so much money on long distance," he said at last.

I practice safe cell phoning by not talking on the phone when I am driving or eating. This includes streamside lunches. No one wants to hear the babble of water intermixed with babble about stock options (not that I have any). You will never find me fondling the melons at Yoke's Grocery while discussing the brown trout bite on the East Fork of the Sevier.

I use barely a third of my cell phone minutes each month, I do not accept incoming calls, I do not talk on the phone where others can hear me, and I do not engage in risky cell phone behavior. You're right—I've no business with one at all.

Winter Tenting

❖❖❖

I was lying on a cot in a large wall tent somewhere in Oregon's high-desert country, wondering if a man ever reaches a point when he doesn't care if he lives or dies. Two friends and I had spent the day casting streamers on an isolated stretch of the Owyhee River, and, with nothing else to do when sunlight and shadows gave way to darkness, we had gone to bed right after camp dinner.

It was cold—below freezing for sure—and as I pulled my thin sleeping bag to my chin, I could see ice crystals floating from my nose each time I exhaled. I'd forgotten a pillow, so my head rested on a near-empty duffel bag with nothing but a spare fly box, a tablet and pen, my shaving kit, and a package of Little Debbie individually wrapped doughnuts for cushioning. The reason the duffel was nearly empty was because I was wearing all the clothes it had held.

My thoughts about dying centered upon a two-burner propane heater in the corner of the tent. With it off, the cold made me ache. Turned on, it would provide enough warmth to let me sleep. But I knew the heater could create enough carbon monoxide to kill everyone in the tent. Die or be cold? Die or be cold? I wondered how the other guys felt about it.

"Whose idea was this, anyway?" I whined. "Who said we would be plenty comfortable in this nice wall tent in the middle of the winter in the middle of a desert? See that hole in the ceiling? That's for the stovepipe. Do you see a woodstove in here anywhere?"

My questions were answered with silence from Jerry and peaceful, resonant snoring from Mike. Both wore only their long underwear. Both had mummy bags guaranteed to 30 below. Both were asleep, dreaming about deep pools and hook-nosed browns.

Already, I had pulled pants and sweatshirt over my long johns. I wore heavy socks on my feet. They hadn't helped. In desperation, I stumbled from the cot to the truck, where I retrieved my chest waders. Though damp outside, they were dry inside, so I slid them on, pulled a ski mask over my head, put on a pair of gloves, and returned to the tent.

"This is going to work," I remember thinking. "I think I'm warming up." I lay there like an overstuffed couch for a full 10 minutes before I had to admit it wasn't working at all. I got up again and pulled a heavy rain jacket over the waders.

When I got back to my cot, Jerry was in full roar, sputtering and gurgling and making all the disgusting nighttime sounds women leave their husbands over. Then Mike joined in with a series of unearthly whistles and grunts. I clomped back to the truck, wedged myself in the backseat in a fetal position, and there I spent the night.

At 6 a.m., there was stirring in the tent. Mike was fixing breakfast just inside the flap, and Jerry was firing up the heater. "So there you are!" Mike said as I stumbled from the truck to stand in front of the glorious warmth. He studied my outfit. "Nice outfit. Did you get cold?" Jerry giggled.

"You know," Jerry said lightly, "I put an extra mummy bag behind the truck seat. You might want to try it out tonight." This time, Mike giggled.

I glared. I knew I should have turned the heater on and killed them both.

Fishing with Claire

"Ganpa?"

"What, Claire?"

"What's that, Ganpa?" I am wandering along a small creek with my 3-year-old granddaughter, just a few blocks from her home in Northern California. Claire carries my fly rod importantly. This was her mother's idea.

Supposedly we are fishing, but really, this is a chance for me to try to be a grandpa. Claire's father, my son, is in the Coast Guard. He is transferred a lot, and in three years, I have seen Claire a total of eight days. His wife thought maybe I could loosen up with my first grandchild if I was in my element.

Claire is pointing to something dark on a rock, and I stoop to study it. "It's a slate drake nymphal shuck," I tell her.

"Oh." Total comprehension. "Ganpa?"

"What, Claire?" I try to be enthused, but being a grandpa is tough for me. Claire is on her knees by a shallow pool. I wince as my fly rod is dropped on the rocks.

"What's that?" This time, her little finger points at a small crayfish.

"It's a crawdad, Claire," I say.

"Catch it."

I drop to my knees. The crawdad scoots away. I look up at Claire apologetically, but she is already wandering back down the path, disinterested. My fly rod is still on the ground.

"Ganpa?" she calls.

"What, Claire?"

"Let's go there." She points to an overgrown trail leading off away from the little creek.

I want to tell her it is a scratchy path to nowhere, but I pick up my old 5-weight and follow obediently. The Grandfather Manual probably has a chapter about not discouraging the adventuresome spirit in a grandchild. Besides, I have been down a few scratchy paths to nowhere myself.

After a few yards, Claire decides she doesn't like the path, and we turn back to the water. "Ganpa?"

"What, Claire?" I sigh. *Was that a rise over by the big rock?*

"Where's Mommy?"

"At home, Claire." *Yeah, I'm pretty sure there's a trout there.* "Do you want to go see Mommy?" I ask absently. "Or do you want to see me catch a fish?" *Hey, that's a pretty decent rainbow for a creek this size!*

"Oooh, catch a fishy, Ganpa," she says enthusiastically.

I make one false cast and drop the little Adams right on the money. The trout sucks it in. "Here, Claire," I say as the fish bolts downstream. "You catch the fishy." I try to hand her the rod, but she squeals and grabs the line instead and heads at a run up the bank.

The trout is jerked ingloriously from the water. I think briefly about trying to release it, but Claire roughly pins it to the rocks. My granddaughter is absolutely beside herself with excitement, and I chuckle at her delighted squeals. She squeezes the 10-inch trout in both hands and holds it toward me, her face aglow with awe and exhilaration.

"Let's show Mommy!" Claire is so wound up she is running in place.

"Okay," I say. "Let's show Mommy."

We cross a muddy spot, and Claire's left foot sinks into the muck.

"It's okay, Ganpa," she says. "It's okay." She hasn't relaxed her grip on the trout.

"You're dirty, kid," I tell her. "Now we have to wash your shoe."

"Why?" she asks.

"Because . . . because I don't know," I say. Why, indeed? It was just something I thought a grandpa should say.

"Ganpa?"

"Yes, Claire?"

"Ganpa, I love you."

"I love you too, Claire." I make a face and she shrieks and runs up the trail clutching our dinner.

Backseats

❖

I know it is the environmentally conscious thing to do, but when friends and I make a long drive to a fly-fishing destination, I am not fond of carpooling. The main problem is, when you ride with someone else, you are sometimes required to ride in the backseat, and though I dearly loved backseats as a teenager, I find them uncomfortable now.

I am tall. Resting my chin on my knees in a small backseat makes my jaw hurt, and my lower back doesn't always straighten out when I get out of the car. Much to the mirth of the other, shorter fellows I fish with, this usually means I need help getting my waders on when we arrive. My friends make terrible jokes and obscene comments while I am writhing on my back. Often, they start fishing without me.

There are other things I do not like about backseats: when I am in the backseat, I cannot hear anyone in the front seat. In order not to appear stupid or aloof, I must smile, grunt, chuckle, or say, "Mmmmm," when they turn and look at me. Saying "Mmmmm" seems to cover the bases more often than not, but I am always afraid I will offend someone by chuckling when they tell me their Aunt Bernie was hit by a train last week.

I think there should be a rule posted in all vehicles that front-seat passengers are allowed to converse only with other front-seat passengers. Backseat passengers should be allowed to stare out the window or sleep. Actually, there should be a rule that no talking whatsoever be allowed in a car. The only thing worse than not being able to hear is being stuck in the back with someone who won't shut up.

I think I'm pretty good at adjusting my conversations to the company I am keeping. On a fly-fishing trip, though, you're supposed to talk about fly fishing. I was stuck in the backseat recently with my brother-in-law, who doesn't fly fish a lick. We were dropping him off at another relative's, who lived on the way. This man takes a lot of enjoyment from all things mechanical. He doesn't just work on cars; he scrounges gears and gaskets and turbulator bearings and builds Ferris wheels and turbines with a five-to-one differential overload capable of generating a thousand foot-pounds of thrust in a dry socket. He knows nothing about fly reels or the merits of synthetic hackle, and I didn't understand a word he said.

When I was going to college, I worked summers for the U.S. Forest Service. I drove a 1950 Chevy sedan I had purchased from my brother-in-law for $35. It was worth less than that, but it did have one redeeming feature—it had no backseat. This, of course, made fathers of my weekend dates a trifle nervous, but it was an economical alternative to a motel when I was fishing the mountain streams.

Halfway through the summer, I found an abandoned outhouse in the woods and resurrected the three-hole sitting board on cinder blocks behind the front seat of my car. I have no idea why I did that, but it seemed hilarious at the time. Unfortunately, it nearly eliminated my ability to get dates, and when I did get one, she always insisted on double-dating with a girlfriend and using someone else's vehicle. This always put me in the backseat. You can see I have been suffering for a long time.

The Error of My Ways

❖

I gained a healthy respect for fire in my single-digit years when friends and I almost burned down the neighbor's garage. It wasn't a malicious act—just dumb. We were shooting wooden matches out of a BB gun, delighting in watching them ignite when they hit a hard surface of the garage. One of them fell in dry cheatgrass, and while we were deciding whether to run or stay, the fire blackened a whole wall and attracted quite a bit of attention.

Later, my father lovingly showed me the error of my ways by lighting his own fire with a belt applied liberally in the vicinity of my back pockets. He told me it hurt him worse than it hurt me, but I seriously doubted the veracity of his confession. What hurt most, though, was that he confiscated my BB gun. And to make sure the lesson stayed with me, he also left me at home to be babysat by my grandmother when he took the rest of the family on our annual summer fly-fishing vacation up north.

Years later, I got a summer job with the U.S. Forest Service on a blister rust crew in Idaho. Firefighting seemed a romantic diversion to a bunch of 18-year olds. Finally flown to our first forest blaze, however, it didn't take long for the romance to wear off. Twelve hours a day on a smoky fire line soon had us remembering with remarkable affection our boring jobs amid the cool forests and sparkling cutthroat creeks in Idaho.

It didn't help, either, that the second night out, while our grimy bodies were wedged into sleeping bags on the hard ground, a wind-blown spark from the nearby conflagration landed in our pile of duffels as we slept, burning everything we had brought with us. Some lost cameras, some transistor radios. My four-piece fly rod burned, as did two paperback books. Left with nothing to pass the evening hours but a jackknife, I created quite a collection of pointed sticks.

Because of the exceptional rainfall this past spring, weeds thrived and grew tall. Then it got hot and dry, and I didn't dare drive to my favorite brown trout water—a small creek in cattle country with nothing but a rutted, overgrown farm road for access. Finally, however, in early September, there was some dew, and I decided the worst of the fire danger had passed.

The trip in was uneventful, though the grass in the middle of the road brushed the undercarriage. The stream was low, but I found a fish quickly on a crawdad imitation. I was just releasing it when I saw smoke. Up the hill from where I had come, flames were licking the weeds in the road. Perhaps it had been a spark from my exhaust. Perhaps, weeds on the undercarriage had combusted.

I raced up the hill. Falling to my knees, I began pushing the flaming debris with my hands into the center of the road, trying to create a ring of bare earth. The whole thing took less than three minutes, but when I could finally relax, my hands were blackened and I could barely get my breath. Pretty certain the threat was over, I nevertheless removed a hubcap from my truck and used it as a vessel to drench the spot with water from the creek.

Driving that truck down there in the dry weeds had been a dumb thing to do—perhaps dumber than shooting matches out of a BB gun. If Dad had been around, he would have been taking off his belt again.

Strange Sightings

I was holed up in a small tent during a late-autumn snowstorm watching my little high-mountain brook trout pond freeze around the edges. As the white powder piled up outside, I was having serious misgivings about hiking so far and staying so long, but fortunately, I had thrown a book into my duffel, and though not as good perhaps as *A Good Life Wasted*, it was a believable and entertaining high-tech adventure. More important, it was something to occupy idle hours until the storm ended and I could hike out without becoming lost.

In one chapter, the book mentioned an incident that occurred in 1947 when a farmer found the wreck of a military spy plane in a field in New Mexico. Much to the military's relief, the media and the public drew the unexpected conclusion it was an alien ship. Newspapers carried the story of the strange find, and public interest hit a fever pitch, but the military denied any knowledge of its secret project. Much better to let the public think aliens were flying above New Mexico than to risk an angry encounter with Russia. Partly as a result of this incident or incidents like it, I grew up hearing all kinds of weird and wonderful stories about outer space aliens.

My grandmother, who went to church regularly, tied a mean Carey Special, didn't drink much, and never told a lie, said she saw a UFO above Moses Lake, Washington, in the late 1950s. If Grams believed it, so did I, and I have since felt that though we had no substantial proof, something could be out there.

We humans want to think there are still undiscovered things capable of mystifying us. But technology is so advanced, there is really nothing I can't imagine. I mean, cell phones are amazing enough. How much more amazed could I be if we perfected time travel or cryogenics or hip waders that didn't leak?

To retain my sense of wonder, I fish. I would much rather watch an otter chase a trout under the clear ice of a mountain river than ponder man's ability to clone a sheep. I far prefer to contemplate the nuances of water over rock than the mysterious innards of a computer.

During my observations of the natural world while fishing, I have seen some exciting stuff—cougars, moose, a two-headed frog, and in a rotten stump, some kind of huge, pasty, corpulent larvae that gave me the creeps. If the babies were that big, I didn't want to see the parents.

A few weeks before my snowstorm adventure, I had one of my most amazing sightings. A friend and I were on Crab Creek south of town. Nymphing had been pretty good for foot-long browns, and we were taking a break on a big boulder beside a dark, basalt-lined pool, when I spotted a creature that neither of us recognized. We walked tentatively toward it. An iguana!

I don't know where iguanas live, but I know they don't reside in the northwest United States. This one was about 3 feet long, had a mouth full of teeth, and when I swished my fly rod at it, it flared a hood around its neck that ballooned up suddenly and caused me to stumble backward.

My friend had numerous theories about how a 3-foot iguana found itself slouching around near our trout stream, but personally, I think it was an alien, probably sent as an ambassador from Pluto to lobby for reinstatement as a planet.

There's a lot of Grams in me yet.

Pat and Me

❖❖❖

Many years ago, I met author Patrick F. McManus. Pat Mc-Manus had been an idol of mine for some time because he wrote humorous outdoor stories I might have written myself had I known how to write.

Pat was teaching night school classes through a local university, so after thinking the situation through very carefully—about eight minutes—I quit my job and went back to school so I could meet him. My soon-to-be ex-wife suggested it may have made more sense to just call him up, but I really wanted to shake his hand.

Pat and I eventually met and even became friends, and he encouraged me to try writing outdoor humor. The way I see it now, he knew he needed a little competition to keep him sharp, and I provided as little as anyone. Still, I have learned to enjoy his company.

In November, Pat and I decided to get together for a Snake River steelhead trip in Idaho's Hells Canyon. Both of us have taken steelhead before, but Pat had never taken one on a fly. Now, I knew that if either of us were to take our own boats into Hells Canyon, neither the boats nor we would ever be seen again. Instead, after calling several numbers and being turned down, I finally booked with an outfitter who didn't know us.

Pat and I had three hours to converse on the way to Hells Canyon. One could probably imagine what two outdoor humorists, both with strong English backgrounds, postgraduate degrees, and considerable fly-fishing experience would talk about on an extended drive. One would be wrong unless one guessed bosoms, microbes, and dog flatulence. Pat, in fact, told me he had recently done an entire column on dog flatulence, and in the next breath he was bemoaning the fact that the general public does not view humorists as "serious" writers.

Over the years, Pat has written numerous columns extolling his ability to not catch fish. As a humorist, he generally delights in disasters, the fodder for most of his articles. He would have liked nothing better than to eventually be able to write in the outfitter's guest book, "Sorry about your boat." And though I didn't want to be part of anything as dramatic as a boat sinking in Hells Canyon, I, too, was hoping for something that would give me a story.

Once we started fishing, I could tell Pat was worried. Sure, there were class IV rapids in the river, but the 28-foot jet sled navigated them with ease. Yes, there had been rain clouds over Spokane when we left, but the weather in the canyon was downright balmy. Pat knew his only chance for a story was to not catch fish, but 30 minutes into the trip, he was already playing a 10-pound steelhead.

"What have you gotten me into, Liere?" he hissed after landing his second fish. "I come all this way, and look, two big fish in the boat—on a fly, fer cryin' out loud—beautiful weather, and no leaks! How do you expect me to get a story out of this?"

I couldn't think of a reply, but an hour later, I set up a picture of my idol holding up a bright, freshly caught hen steelhead. Just as I pushed the shutter, the fish flipped in Pat's arms and the tail slapped him in the face, "sliming" his tasteful fly-fishing vest from top to bottom and knocking his porkpie hat askew. If a picture is worth a thousand words, at least I got my story.

I Don't Want to Be a Guide

❧

I used to think I would like to be a fishing guide, but life dictated I would be a schoolteacher instead; I won't go into the details. Teaching pretty much made me miserable for 30 years, but it was steady work and climate controlled, and I had my weekends and my summers and my sick leave.

I have fished with a fair number of guides, and I've decided guiding for a living could be much like teaching for a living if you let it: it could eventually become work, perhaps even hateful work, and you could lose sight of the things that attracted you to the profession in the first place.

Last year, I fished Washington's Grande Ronde River for steelhead with a guide named Darrin. The way Darrin went about it, steelheading was a lot of work. For starters, we met at 4 a.m. That meant I had to get up at 3 a.m. When I was 19, I got up at 3 all the time, but it was in the afternoon, which probably explains why it took me six years to finish college. Forty years later, 3 a.m. is still an unreasonable time to be awake. Three a.m. is dark, and dark is for sleeping. One should not be poking around in the garage at 3:15 a.m. looking for a fly vest. Packing a lunch before you've even had breakfast is not right. And to think—a steelhead guide does it morning after morning after morning.

The three-hour drive down was pleasant enough, but once we had launched his drift boat on the river, Darrin changed. The river was high, and he was trying to maneuver a boat in a fast current using nothing but oars and back muscles. There was urgency, for once we passed a good steelhead spot, we could not fish it again.

"Cast there! Cast there!" he would scream as we went ripping by a pool.

I would cast.

"Not there, not there!" he screamed. "Cast next to the rock." But it seemed to me that, from a swiftly moving boat, "next to" was a matter of perspective.

"Ah !#%@*!" Darrin would say. "Never mind. We missed it."

Being new to this kind of fishing, I missed my cast on several occasions or wedged my fly in the rocks. This caused us to "lose" a lot of water, and Darrin seemed to take it personally. He was practically crying when I cast short into what he said was his favorite pool and the boat swept through without a hit.

Darrin complained that I was missing strikes, though I had felt nothing that resembled a strike. He also had a fit when I quit casting for a moment and tried to grab a bite of my lunch. After three hours, I was starving. I get a little cranky myself when I am starving.

"Son," I said at last, "I've never fished this river before. It's beautiful and challenging—exactly what I'd hoped for—but to tell the truth, right now I don't much care if I catch a fish or not."

Darrin looked at me as if I had just propositioned him. "We've got to catch a fish," he sniveled.

I studied him sympathetically. "Darrin," I said, "I've never cared about the fish as much as the experience. I spent a lot of time in my life being miserable, but I was getting paid for it. I'm sure as hell not paying someone to make me that way again. Now, if you'll just pull onto the next gravel bar and hand me that red cooler... It's way past my lunchtime, son, and I may even have myself a little snooze. I'd suggest you do the same."

Giving Gifts

———— ⟋⟍ ————

I really could have used insulated socks and insulated underwear for Christmas. When my children asked, that's what I told them. I figured it would be easier to remember than Korkers wading shoes with the new OmniTrax V2 interchangeable sole system. But once the Christmas presents were unwrapped, there was not a pair of socks or underwear in the bunch. No wading shoes, either.

I hate it when someone asks me what I want for Christmas or a birthday. When I was small and optimistic that wasn't the case, but I discovered early on that the things I really wanted—like puppies and chemistry sets—were never received. I wasted a lot of good lap time telling Santa about my wish for a beagle. I also learned that if I wanted a chemistry set, I'd best not use the phrase "blowing things up" during the request.

Once, because I was asked, I composed an elaborate wish list and handed it out to inquiring relatives, but nothing good came of it. Somehow, my wish for fly rods and vests and vises metamorphosed into robes and slippers and soap on a rope.

When I must shop for a gift, I find that the perfect one comes only after much suffering: I'll never find it at the first store. A perfect Christmas gift must be searched for on a crowded, drizzly Saturday when there are no parking spaces anywhere, the snowbanks are 10 feet tall, and I am giving up a winter fly-fishing trip. The perfect gift must jump out at me, speak to me—not like a rubber singing fish, but as a stirring in my heart.

A perfect gift to give must be unique yet practical; unpretentious but not cheap. It must reflect insight into the personality of both recipient and giver. When someone opens a perfect gift, he or she will not say, "Oh, you shouldn't have!" No, the recipient will light up, then linger over it, forgetting all other gifts in the need to try a false cast or two.

Perfect gifts are unexpected, because the recipient didn't realize he had to have it until he saw it. Then he wonders how he did without for so long. I have received a few perfect gifts during my 62 years, beginning with a clown punching bag when I was 8 years old. Another perfect gift was the insulated denim jacket/shirt I received from my son and daughter-in-law. I've had that thing eight years now, and it is still my go-to garment each winter morning. It is warm, rugged, faded, frayed, and stained with blood, fly dressing, bacon grease, and wood smoke, but when I put that jacket on, my world is right—it is an extension of who I am.

My daughter gave me a perfect gift for Valentine's Day when she was 8 years old, but I doubt that she even remembers giving it to me. It was a simple wooden clothespin on which she had glued a paper butterfly she had drawn, cut out, and colored. On the other side was a paper heart with the message, "To my very special daddy."

I think what I'm going to do next Christmas is hand out lists of the things I do not want. This would include anything made of plastic, vinyl, wicker, polyester, or natural ingredients. It would also include things that need assembly, make noise, or hang on walls collecting dust.

And if anyone is paying attention—you couldn't go wrong with an Orvis Superfine Trout Bum Rod.

Putting in Time

◆

A friend and I were recently quite a ways from home, casting black marabou flies off a city dock for small crappie. As anglers are inclined to do, we struck up a conversation with a gentleman fishing next to us, and he was surprised we had driven so far to fish.

"It was something to do," my friend, Mike, replied, and I nodded.

On the way home, I got to thinking about what Mike had said. Was that it—something to do—the reason we had driven so far to spend a blustery morning casting for 9-inch crappie?

Mike had retired just recently, but I have been retired for almost five years. I'd never really thought about my leisure-time activities as merely "something to do." After all these years as a productive citizen, am I now only putting in time? After 40 years in the work-force, 40 years raising a family, accumulating, scrimping, saving, going out on a limb and over my head, doing all the things one must do to get from there to here, was my life now reduced to finding things to occupy the hours?

Let's see, I thought. What else could I have done this morning? Well, I could have fertilized the lawn or repaired the porch swing or filled ruts in the driveway or replaced the missing shingles on the shed roof. I could have fixed my daughter's gate and hauled an accumulation of her winter residue to the dump. I could have dug and transplanted the raspberries I said I'd give her, rototilled her flowerbeds, and finished building the doghouse I started two months ago.

I guess I could have volunteered a few hours at the church or put up a basketball standard for the grandkids, and I know I've been meaning to catch up on my Spanish correspondence course, and practice my harmonica more faithfully.

But as we left town, a calf moose had galloped awkwardly down the center of the highway and disappeared into a clump of willows. Farther along, we passed a big slough covered with white pelicans, and every scab-rock pond from that point on was filled with pintails, wigeons, and mallards, and all their skittering offspring.

We passed a field of winter wheat jammed with Canada geese, and as we dropped into the last canyon before the lake, wild turkeys and deer dotted the hillsides. Pretty soon, we were in sight of the water, and we turned at a big T, and headed toward the south end. On the left side of the road, steep, rugged, basalt cliffs seemed to drop from the sky, and every mile or so a new spring waterfall plunged from somewhere up there cascading from one shelf to another in a misty spray that eventually settled in deep, green plunge pools next to the road.

Meanwhile, on the right side of the road, the lake slid along beside us. We soon observed bald eagles swooping, soaring, and diving in to pluck unidentified fish from the water. The big birds sat in twos and threes on snags and cliff edges, and it was comical to see how their low, majestic flights over the bays sent huge flocks of coots scurrying frantically across the water. Mike said the coots looked like they were running on their toes across hot coals.

Putting in time? I don't think so. When I was putting in the hours long ago, going about the business of life, I always had a vision. It looked very much like my recent fishing trip for 9-inch crappie.

A Lotta Bull!

❖

In early April, Mike Sweeney and I were prospecting for rainbows on Wyoming's North Platte River when a thunderstorm liquefied a big piece of the high mountain snow pack and sent it roaring by us in a foamy chocolate torrent. We retreated to my camper, optimistically determined to wait it out, but after a couple of hours, the river had only gotten higher and muddier, and the camper was rocking from wind gusts of more than 40 miles per hour. Bored, Mike brewed some new coffee while I thumbed through a paper we had picked up in Casper the night before. It looked like a long afternoon.

"Hey!" I said as I turned the pages. "There's a Western art show in Casper this afternoon."

"Not interested," Mike said dryly.

"How 'bout a four-family yard sale?" I asked. "It says there's lots of fishing stuff."

"I don't need any more stuff," Mike said. "What I need is another good 5-weight."

"Well, what about this one?" I persisted. "There's a bull auction at the fairgrounds in a couple of hours. We could buy us a Cheshire and have a barbecue."

"I don't think Cheshires are bulls," Mike said. "I think Cheshire's a type of horse—like a hopaloosa."

"Whatever," I told him. "But it looks like we're done fishing for awhile, and I've tied enough flies to last a couple of years. I think a bull auction would be fun."

Mike disagreed, but I was driving, so we arrived together at the fairgrounds 10 minutes before the auction began. Though Mike stubbornly remained in the camper, I went inside, took a seat in a row of bleachers, and tried to make sense of the goings-on. Most of the shoptalk I didn't understand, but I did gather that there are three things one looks for when bidding on a bull: size of its rump, size of its belly, and size of its testicles.

The auctioneer was amazing. The first bull, a Hereford, I believe he said, looked to me to have a very adequate set of testicles, but the auctioneer also mentioned other things I had failed to notice: "Lotta pigment in the eyes, boys, lotta pigment," he'd say, or, "Lotta loin, lotta loin." That bull sold for more than $2,000, so I knew right away I wasn't going to be bidding on the makings for a barbecue.

"Look at the spread, boys, look at the spread," the auctioneer chanted, pausing so everyone could take this attribute, whatever it was, into consideration. Then he resumed his calling, and by golly—the price on the next bull went even higher. It, too, had nice testicles, I thought. In fact, it looked exactly like the bull that had chased me across Fenton's Pasture when I was casting poppers for bluegill in the old man's farm pond.

I didn't stay for the entire auction, but I hung around long enough to see one big, black Angus, which appeared to have some excellent dubbing material on his flanks, sell for $7,000. Once again, the auctioneer did a masterful job of getting the bidding higher when it seemed to have stalled. The seven grand seemed a lot to pay for dubbing.

All in all, I'm glad I went—and not just because it was pouring buckets outside and the North Platte was way too brown to fish. It was refreshing to be in a room full of nice folks, all with a passion for something that goes back to our roots. No loud music, no iPods, no freaky hair or pierced eyebrows, and darn few cell phones. I've had a lot less fun when I'm not fishing.

Friends

❖

I have known Mike for 30 years. Recently, I dug out an old picture of him, a photo of a dark-headed young man holding a fly rod and a stringer of big crappie. I wish I could remember when and where the photo was taken, because Mike's hair turned white quite a few fishing seasons ago, and we haven't caught a crappie more than 8 inches long on a fly for years. You'd think I'd remember 14-inch crappie. The fact is, though, our most memorable outings are the ones when things don't all go right—like our recent cold weather fishing trip to Montana.

Sometimes Mike and I let our dogs, Sis and Leah, tag along when we go fly fishing. They are good about staying out of our drifts, and my Labrador, Sis, gave up helping me land fish several years ago when she got a size-10 Adams embedded in her nose. Leah mostly just appreciates being in Mike's presence.

The lady at the motel in Montana was reluctant to let us keep our dogs in the room. "We've had some issues," she told us.

Mike and I assured her that our labs had stayed in many motels and were 100 percent housebroken. They knew they weren't allowed on beds. Finally, the lady relented.

The first night in the motel, Mike got up to use the bathroom. Suddenly, there was a curse, the light came on, and he was clumping across the room on his heels.

"What's going on?" I asked sleepily.

"Your dog crapped on the carpet and I stepped in it!" he said angrily as he reached the bathroom door.

"Sis doesn't do that," I said defensively.

"Neither does Leah," he countered.

"Well, maybe it was you," I suggested. "You know how you sleepwalk."

"Very funny," Mike said in a tone that let me know it was not.

After he cleaned his foot, Mike and I scrubbed the carpet as best we could. Six hours later, we got up and went fishing. Back in town, we stopped at the store and split the cost of rug cleaner, deodorizer, and a scrub brush. At the motel, however, the lady at the front desk had already been in our room and was not very happy, so Mike and I split the $50 she said it would take to have the carpet professionally cleaned.

The next afternoon, far out of town on a rutted dirt road, Mike and I and the dogs returned from the river to find that the keys were locked in Mike's truck.

"Why would you leave the keys in the ignition?" I asked.

"I always leave the keys in the ignition," Mike explained. "I didn't think you'd press the 'lock' button on your way out."

"I didn't press the lock button," I said.

It was cold, we were wet and hungry, and our tempers could have erupted, but instead, Mike and I twisted a piece of wire off a sagging fence and made a small loop in the end. With me prying the top corner of the door open with a lug wrench wrapped in toilet paper, Mike inserted the wire, fished around for a few minutes, and popped the lock.

Mike and I enjoyed pretty decent fishing in Montana. The scenery was breathtaking, food in the little café was excellent, and we both made some great casts. And in a few years, all will be forgotten but the mess on the carpet and the keys locked in the truck. Those are the stories we will tell our grandchildren.

For a 20-Pound Pike

❖❖❖

It was the end of my last day at the large lake in northern Saskatchewan, and my guide, Ed, was fiddling with the outboard motor while I reluctantly stowed my fly rods in their cases. By conservative estimate, I had caught and released 80 pike in three days, throwing everything from poppers to giant streamers, and though I hadn't caught the 20-pounder of my dreams, I was happy. Far down the lake a warm lodge and a big steak awaited me.

Just ahead, I could see three other boats from the same lodge. They were randomly motoring back and forth across a wide bay along the edge of an ice flow. When we had entered the bay that morning it had been clear, but the wind had since shifted, and now a huge, rotten slab of ice clogged our passage. A few tantalizing openings into the heart of the ice field offered false hope, but all these ended shy of open water, and shifting wind could trap a venturesome boat within a foot-thick mass of grinding, pulsating ice.

We motored closer, and to my horror, one of the guides decided to be hero for the day, plunging his craft and his passenger deep into one of these openings. The guide was mine. In an instant, we were 40 yards into the middle of an angry ice flow; there was no outlet, and the inlet was closing behind us. I heard a terrible gnashing noise. "The boat is breaking up!" I yelled.

"You're grinding your teeth," Ed replied. "Hand me a life vest, will ya?" Then he grinned a silly grin. "Course, a life vest ain't gonna do much good in water this cold, is it?"

Ed goosed the engine in forward, then reverse, rocking the plywood boat to break it free. When the engine choked and died, only the tinkling and grinding of the glimmering ice could be heard. Anglers in the other boats outside the flow sat helplessly and watched.

I grabbed an oar and tried to keep opposing cakes of ice from cracking us like a walnut. "I wanted to be shot at age 90 by a jealous husband," I whined as I frantically pushed small icebergs aside. "This isn't the way I wanted to die!"

Even Ed, a veteran of many North Country ice-outs, looked worried.

Finally, miraculously, we worked our plywood boat free of the grinding flow, though our path home was still blocked by the frozen mass. Somehow, however, being late for dinner now seemed no more than an inconvenience. Everyone pulled into shore. We built a huge fire, gathered close, and prepared to spend the night. Rain fell intermittently and it turned colder, but the fire was warm and the conversation good. We were dressed well, and we had fish and snacks in the boats if anyone got too hungry.

The wind began four hours later, and the ice made a soft tinkling sound as it began to move. Then it took on the roar of heavy traffic. The huge sheet gained momentum, moving faster and faster. It began racing down lake, pushing up in 5-foot piles on the points, crashing and popping and ripping a passage to the open water.

Ed had the outboard running again, and we wasted no time making our escape. "Home" was still 45 minutes away. There would be steak, and all of us would talk and laugh and share our insights and perhaps drink a toast to good friends, great adventure, and the promise of next year. What, after all, was a little inconvenience to the possibility of a 20-pound pike on a fly?

It Should Be There

———— ⁕ ————

I am not good at finding things. Possibly this is because I am not good at putting things away. Lacey, in fact, told me I never put anything away. This is a gross exaggeration, because just last week I took a bag full of fly-tying materials and put it away with my own two hands. But I can't remember where. It should be in the hackle drawer of my plastic storage bin, or at the very least in the one labeled "MISCELLANEOUS FLY STUFF." It isn't, though. Eventually, Lacey will find it and then she'll tell me again I never put anything away. It's a vicious circle.

Lacey is uncanny about finding things. She thinks it is her responsibility as a female to help me locate items I have lost or misplaced—part of her job description. Sometimes I will be rummaging around in my den, cursing slightly under my breath, and Lacey, from the living room where she is ensconced in a novel, will look up and say, "What are you looking for?"

"Nothing," I'll say.

She will then stare at me for a long second or two. "Try the drawer under the corkboard," she'll suggest. I will, and nine times out of 10, that's where I'll find my tying vise. It only works if *she* tells me to look there, however. If I look there first by myself, Lacey will eventually find it in the attic mixed in with the Thanksgiving decorations.

If I tell Lacey I am looking for my new Ross reel, she'll ask me when I used it last.

"When I fished Beryl Creek with Mike," I'll say.

"OK," Lacey will sigh, getting out of her chair and walking slowly through the den, touching various closet doors and cupboards. "That means it's got to be behind the door with the landing net and the waders." She will stop and extract my reel from where I never, ever, put anything but landing nets and waders. I think she can feel vibrations.

Lacey is particularly good at finding keys, wallets, and polarized sunglasses, because I leave them in predictable places. She also has an uncanny ability to run the day's events backward in her mind until she arrives at the precise moment an item disappeared. From there, it is one more easy step backward to locate the hiding place. One item that gave her problems, however, was my bear whistle.

In the winter, I referee girls' eighth-grade junior varsity basketball. I use the same whistle I carry year-round to minimize contact with large hairy bruins that want the same fishing pool that I do. When I showed up at the gym to call my second game of the year, I couldn't find that whistle anywhere. I called my wife.

"When did you use it last?" she asked.

"I had it last week when I ran out to the Seneca River after calling that game at Fanning Junior High."

"What were you wearing at the game?"

"You know I wear the same pants and shirt the entire season."

"Oh yes I do," she replied. "I've heard the complaints. Did you look in the shirt pocket?"

"Yes, yes, yes," I told her impatiently. "I looked in all the obvious places."

"Well, then," Lacey said, "the whistle has to be in one of your tennis shoes."

"But, Lacey," I complained, "I'm wearing my tennis shoes."

"How do they feel?" she asked innocently.

Silence.

"I'll see you in a couple hours, darling," Lacey said. "I hope your foot feels better."

Scary Things

W hen I was a kid, I was fascinated by quicksand. Usually, there was at least one good batch of it in every Tarzan movie, and it was always saved for the final scene when the bad guys, thinking they were getting away, stumbled into this soupy horror and perished.

Much later, I learned that the "quicksand" of the movies was actually a combination of oatmeal and water, and that real quicksand is actually a fairly rare commodity. Though I was disappointed to learn this, I thought making something as fun as quicksand out of oatmeal was a pretty good use for my least favorite breakfast food.

I have never been in quicksand, but I have been in mud up to my knees, and it was a terrifying situation, as I was also in water up to my chest. I had been fly fishing a beaver pond a long way from nowhere when I got stuck. Whenever I struggled, I went deeper in the mud, so I decided early on that if I had to, I would stand there without further movement until I starved to death. Fortunately, my fishing partner rescued me before that happened, but I must tell you, the incident ranks as number two on the list of the most fear-evoking things in my life.

Oddly enough, the very scariest thing also occurred when I was fly fishing. That time, a man held a .22 rifle to my head while his wife screamed at him to shoot me. It happened like this:

Three of us had decided to take advantage of the mayfly hatch on a secluded and little-known stream up north. We knew a man who owned some property on the creek, and he had given us a key to his gate. After fishing all afternoon, we were on our way back to the car when an armed man, his armed wife, and his five armed children, all under age 10, confronted us. The first thing he said as I came into sight was, "Who you related to?"

I thought this a rather peculiar question.

"Who *you* related to?" I questioned. I thought perhaps he knew me.

"Don't get smart with me, bub!" the man roared. "Yer trespassin'."

"Shoot him! Shoot him!" his wife suggested. "Ain't nothin' but a smart-alecky kid." Her five armed children started waving their rifles.

"Now wait a minute," I said, stepping toward the man. "We've got a key..."

"Hold 'er right there, bub," the man said, putting the rifle against my forehead.

Holding 'er right there seemed like an excellent thing to do.

After a lot of negotiating, I came to the conclusion the whole lot of them were a few fries shy of a Happy Meal. I can't say this realization made me feel any better. The man said they owned the land and someone was trying to steal it from them. He lowered the gun, but his eyes were wild, and I could tell he'd been drinking.

Finally, after we apologized profusely for trespassing, promised to never return, and expressed sympathy for his dilemma, we got in my car. As we roared away, one of my friends, Larry, stuck his head out the window and yelled a parting obscenity. I wish he had waited just a bit longer, as one bullet hit my side mirror and another hit a tire. I drove 12 miles with a flat, but it seemed prudent to put some space between us.

Once we hit the highway, I let Larry change the tire. He told me he'd only been scared more two or three times in his life. Obviously, he fly fished more than I.

For 40 years, Alaska was my dream destination. However, having just completed my ninth fly-fishing trip there—five by camper, one by ferry, and three by air—I'm searching for a different dream: familiarity, contempt, and all that.

Anticipation, as they say, is half the fun. There's probably much in Alaska I haven't experienced, but as far as fly fishing goes, I'm content.

I've driven every mile of every highway in the state—from Tok to Prudhoe Bay on the Arctic Ocean, from Eagle to Homer on the Pacific. I've visited Chicken, Manley Hot Springs, Talkeetna, Ninilchik, and North Pole. I've cast flies on the Iliamna, the Kenai, the Russian, the Gulkana, the Kuskokwim, and Tangle Lake. I've paid $14 for a mediocre hamburger and $4 for a Diet Pepsi in a can. I've paid $6 a gallon for gas.

The first three times I drove to Alaska, it was glorious adventure; now the Alaska Highway is paved all the way from Dawson Creek to Delta Junction. If you go, however, and feel you are missing some of the adventure because of the asphalt, take the "unimproved" road that runs north out of Seward to Resurrection Bay. In midsummer, you can wade and cast streamers there for huge coho salmon and Dolly Varden char. But the short drive is a rutted, potholed minefield that has claimed two of my trailer axles and a windshield in four trips.

On my last trip up north the Stewart-Cassiar Highway had washed out, so I was forced to forgo pike fishing plans in the Yukon and drive the Alaska Highway back. I saw bears, ptarmigan, foxes, bison, moose, loons, eagles, and stone sheep, but having seen bears, ptarmigan, foxes, bison, moose, loons, eagles, and stone sheep before, I found myself wishing I could read a book while someone else drove.

I know these are very un-Alaskan observations. If I do go again, I will probably be met at the border by a lynch mob from various departments of tourism as well as all the jade, gold, and fur peddlers in the state. The log Alaska "cache" has lost its intrigue, as have dogsled rides (on rubber-tire-equipped "sleds"), carved sheep horns, and dried ungulate turds made into earrings and bracelets.

I don't want to fish for halibut ever again, either—even with a fly. Catching a halibut on a fly is a lot of work, even with a fly rod that looks very much like a broomstick. A 12-inch brookie on a 4-weight fly rod is a lot more fun. Another thing I do not want to ever do again in Alaska is go on a chartered cruise on Prince William Sound. I always wanted to see a killer whale, a blue iceberg, and a sea otter up close. Now that I have, I don't need to see them again, especially if the "tour" puts me on the water for nine hours without a fly rod, much of that time spent looking at fog.

On my last three-week trip to Alaska, I caught grayling, sheefish, four species of salmon, rainbow trout, and Dolly Varden. I ate fish 11 times for dinner. Mostly this was because hamburger was $5 a pound and milk was almost $10 a gallon. At night, I lay awake waiting for the mosquitoes in my camper to have their way with me.

As with anything, the first time is usually the best. I don't dislike Alaska; I'm merely satiated. I think you should go, however. Lord knows it's a glorious adventure the first eight times around.

A Good Day Indeed

◆

I was supposed to blow out the sprinkler lines on Sunday, but Saturday night I was praying Sunday would be cold and windy, and it was. It is easy to convince yourself the sprinkler lines don't need blowing if they're already frozen.

My prayer wasn't a long one—barely more than a quiet moment, really. I am of the opinion that long prayers are best done in church by experts, or by brothers-in-law at the dinner table on Thanksgiving. I don't feel comfortable with long prayers. "Thanks for the day, God," is my favorite benediction. I use it a lot on weekends during fishing season.

Sometimes in the summer when I want to take the float tube out to Amber Lake, I pray for good weather, but in December I like it more unsettled. When it is cold and the wind is blowing, the big rainbows cruise the shallow water on Lake Roosevelt, and I can sometimes find them within casting distance of shore.

I got up early Sunday, drank three cups of coffee, and read the paper. Then my wife, Lacey, asked me if I wanted breakfast—bacon, fresh eggs, and hotcakes. Ever mindful of getting my recommended daily allowance of cholesterol, I said I did. Afterward, I had one last cup of coffee and finished the newspaper. By then, it was 8 a.m., and the wind had really picked up. I decided I needed to stack some wood before I headed out.

Lacey was already outside, trying to roll up the stiff garden hoses, but when she saw me stacking, she offered to help. Lacey suffers from the "Little Red Hen" syndrome and cannot stand to let me be solely responsible for putting up the year's wood supply. She says she could not enjoy the fires of winter if she knew she hadn't helped. Fortunately, I do not feel the same way about rolling up hoses.

With both of us working, I still had time on my hands after

stacking the wood, so I took the Labrador pup for a walk down to the pond. To my delight, she charged boldly into the water on the first throw, retrieved the stick to hand, and pranced about enthusiastically waiting for me to toss another.

When we got back to the house, I gathered my fly-fishing gear and put some water and an apple in a red fanny pack. I drove to a parking spot above the lake and took my time going down to the water. I had pussyfooted only 200 yards when a red-tailed hawk flew over, screeching that breathy screech.

I had stopped as I always do to admire its graceful flight, when to my left, I caught an image that seemed out of place. Forty yards away, a cougar with a tail as big around as a coffee mug stared at me from atop a large, lone, rounded boulder that curved up like the back of a whale from the forest floor. Even as I began to gasp, it whirled and disappeared.

I think I was more thrilled than frightened, but suddenly, the forest ahead looked terribly dark. I turned and retraced my steps to the truck. Then the sun peeked through, and I sat on the tailgate, breaking pieces off a nearby mullein stalk and soaking up the warmth. There would be no baked trout that evening, but I knew I had experienced something even greater. "Thanks for the day, God." I said. It seemed more inadequate than usual.

What's Your Passion?

———— ✦ ————

Once I accepted the fact I would never be an auto mechanic, an electrician, a cabinetmaker, or even someone who could hang a picture without major injury, my life became much simpler. There are some things I do well, perhaps better than the next fellow. So instead of risking blunt-object trauma, familial hostility, or arrest, I do what I do and hire someone to do what I don't, which is almost everything that has to do with tools.

Although my father was fairly handy, his son is not. Dad could follow written instructions; I cannot. Dad had a logical way of looking at things to see how they must work; I do not. I was given one of those children's tool chests when I was quite small—the ones with the plastic hammer and screwdriver and saw—and it took me three hours to figure out how to open the thing. Once I did, I had two emergency-room visitations before my dad decided plastic was too dangerous for me.

When I became a parent of my own, I bought my son a child's tool chest, but he quickly became bored with it. He was much more interested in trying to take apart my best fly reel with the only three tools I owned—a hammer, a screwdriver, and a saw. I knew I had spawned a throwback to Dad when he asked if I had a small Allen wrench and some vise grips. He wanted a socket set for his fifth birthday. He got my reel apart, and—even more amazing—he put it back together again.

There has been a lot of buzz lately about the "complete man." Supposedly, someone wrote a book about it, and people are actually buying into the concept of completeness. The complete man, says the book, can whip up a soufflé, weld aluminum, make a tasteful flower arrangement, balance the books, and repair a water pump. He makes his children proud, his wife happy, and his dogs obedient. He can sing, dance, golf in the 70s, rope a steer, install storm windows, and raise prize-winning dahlias. There's nothing in there about his ability to tie a size-16 Green Olive or fish it effectively, however.

The book would have you believe that happiness cannot be achieved without completeness. I would have you believe this is hogwash. Happiness is achieved by finding something, perhaps just one thing, you like and doing it. You don't even have to do it well, as long as it gives you pleasure and you stick to it.

I know people who are Detroit Lions fans and a fair number who love the Chicago Cubs. That's what they do. Their loyalty never wavers; their enthusiasm never diminishes. They are no great shakes, perhaps, as fathers, husbands, or breadwinners. They may bowl in the low double digits, but they have found something they are good at—rooting for losing teams.

I am actually a pretty poor fly fisherman if you count only the mechanics of tying flies and casting, but piscatorial pursuits with feather and chenille afford me much pleasure. I stalk trout with passion; I study their waters and their food sources, look for them in the off-season, know where they go and when they go there.

I have friends whose casting mechanics are even worse than mine, whose dry flies look like the bottom of a wren's nest. But they like fly fishing every bit as much as I do. Proficiency, thank God, isn't a prerequisite to passion. If it were, I'd have to stay home.

Exit Laughing

◆

My best friend, Eddie, died last week. Though only 63 years old, he had been in a nursing home for a long time after having a stroke. For a while he seemed poised for recovery, but he soon began a four-year downward spiral complicated by cancer and diabetes. His death was a blessing.

Eddie loved to laugh, whether at himself or others. He was particularly fond of slapstick humor. A good joke would make him giggle, but should you fall off a log while casting to brown trout on Chimikain Creek, he would almost explode. His laughs came from deep inside, ricocheting around his innards before blasting to freedom in a momentous roar.

Eddie and I used to wander around farm country looking for unlikely fishing holes in the scabrock region south of town. After a few hours of casting, Eddie would get bored and get to poking around in one of the old barns that was invariably close by.

On one of these exploratory trips, I stayed below while Eddie climbed a ladder and creaked around above me in the loft. Every time he took a step, the floor sagged, and I was just about to yell at him to come down when he came crashing through in an explosion of planks, dust, feathers, and dried pigeon droppings.

Eddie had the wind knocked from him, and his mouth was full of debris. He landed sitting up, and from where I stood, I thought the darkness around his mouth was blood. He'd also landed on the new 4-weight rod he'd leaned against the wall. Nevertheless, I could not stop laughing. I think it was there I learned about the fine line between tragedy and humor.

Pretty soon, an odd sound welled up in Eddie's throat, and I thought for sure he was a goner. Then he began spitting dried pigeon droppings and straw, and a tremendous laugh reverberated throughout the barn. When Eddie finally got his wind back, he was laughing at himself!

On another expedition, Eddie and I were casting nymphs in a little creek when he got his foot wedged between a stump and some rocks. When I came upon him, he was thrashing horribly. With a mighty roar and a violent jerk, he freed himself by ripping his feet clear of his tennis shoes and then tumbling sideways into the water. Once again, I laughed immediately and he laughed later.

On a camping/fishing trip with Eddie and another friend, Mike, Eddie stayed in camp one night while Mike and I looked for roadkill rattlesnakes. We planned to make some hatbands from the skins. We put our smashed rattlesnakes in a paper sack and returned to camp, where we left the sack on a picnic table. The next morning, Mike extended the sack to Eddie and asked him if he wanted some pepperoni. When Eddie reached in and came out with a headless snake, his terrified shouts shattered the windows of the ranger station a half mile away, and Mike and I hurt ourselves laughing. A few hours later, though, Eddie had the last laugh when Mike accidentally wrapped an anchor rope around his foot and threw himself into the lake. Fortunately, we were looking for crappie in shallow water.

Life with Eddie did, indeed, provide a lot of mirth, and after it all, he had the last laugh at my expense. His family buried him with his favorite 6-weight, and Eddie knew how I coveted that rod. Then I slipped on the ice and fell flat on my back while helping carry his casket across an icy parking lot to the hearse.

See ya later, pal.

Alan Liere, a lifelong resident of Eastern Washington, is an award-winning humor columnist for *Wildfowl*, *Northwest Fly Fishing*, *Southwest Fly Fishing*, *Eastern Fly Fishing*, *Petersen's Hunting*, and *The Upland Almanac* magazines. He has published thousands of articles in dozens of regional and national publications and several papers. Graduated twice from Eastern Washington University, once with a BA in education and again with an MFA in nonfiction writing, Liere taught in the Mead School District for 30 years until retirement released him from his misery. He is a member of the Northwest Outdoor Writers Association, Outdoor Writers Association of America, Safari Club International, Ducks Unlimited, and National Rifle Association.

Although he describes himself as an "avid outdoor enthusiast," Liere admits that perhaps "zealot hunting and fishing nutcake" is closer to the truth. Proof of this is his peculiar passion for chukar hunting and stream fishing. Says Liere, "I am basically a very unlucky person. Over the years, I have perfected both the flinch and the long-line release. I'd probably be a lot better off with a set of golf clubs, but I find the thought revolting."

Liere began writing for magazines in 1981. Since then, he has published three collections of outdoor humor, *Bear Heads and Fish Tales* (1988), *And Pandemonium Rained* (1997), and *Dancin' With Shirley* (1999). This fourth collection is long overdue.